WONDERS OF MAN

TEOTIHUACÁN

by Karl E. Meyer

and the Editors
of the Newsweek Book Division

NEWSWEEK, New York

NEWSWEEK BOOK DIVISION

JOSEPH L. GARDNER   *Editor*

Janet Czarnetzki   *Art Director*

Jonathan Bartlett   *Associate Editor*
Laurie P. Winfrey   *Picture Editor*
Kathleen Berger   *Copy Editor*

S. ARTHUR DEMBNER   *Publisher*

WONDERS OF MAN

MILTON GENDEL   *Consulting Editor*

Mary Ann Joulwan   *Designer, Teotihuacán*

Grateful acknowledgment is made for permission
to quote on page 87 from *The Aztecs: People
of the Sun* by Alfonso Caso, translated by Lowell
Dunham, copyrighted 1958 by the University of
Oklahoma Press and from *The Rise and Fall of
Maya Civilization* by J. Eric Thompson, copyright 1954 by the University of Oklahoma Press,
on page 72.

ISBN: Clothbound Edition 0–88225–083–3
ISBN: Deluxe Edition 0–88225–084–1
Library of Congress Catalog Card No. 73–87151
© 1973 — Arnoldo Mondadori Editore, S.p.A.

Contents

Introduction

Abandoned for twelve hundred years, Teotihuacán stands today as mute testimony to the genius of its unknown creators. The sprawling complex, begun around 100 B.C. on the dusty tableland north of modern Mexico City, was both the first metropolis in the Americas and a remarkable example of city planning. At its height, Teotihuacán encompassed some 2,600 major structures, including markets and apartment compounds clustered along spacious esplanades. A city of temples, it was dominated by two majestic altars set atop opposing pyramids. Its population was greater than that of Periclean Athens, and it exercised loose suzerainty over all of central Mexico and Honduras — the region scholars know as Mesoamerica. Then, in the middle of the eighth century, the inhabitants of Teotihuacán abandoned their capital. With only the wondrous city to bear them witness, an entire people stepped out of the pages of history.

Who were these people? Where did they come from? What role did they play? To be at all comprehensible, the answers to these questions must be viewed against the background of Mesoamerican prehistory — against the rise of such civilizations as the Olmec, Maya, Toltec, Mixtec, and Aztec; and against the terrible moment when European firearms abruptly ended this long cultural tradition.

The tracing and reconstruction of these civilizations has been a long and engrossing study, as the ensuing narrative makes clear. Much of our knowledge has been gained by chance, from the hunches and observations of quirky, self-educated adventurers who sought historic sites in places where scientists knew they could not be. Much of our understanding has also come from the painstaking archaeological spadework of these same scientists. When all the artifacts, all the observations, and all the intuitions are combined, they yield a story that is more in keeping with detective fiction than sober reality. Clues have been culled from jungle and laboratory alike — and when pieced together they tell a story of unusual richness in surprising detail. Not all the answers are available, but scholarly sleuths are nonetheless able to paint a fair likeness of the remarkable civilizations that arose in Mesoamerica in the millennium preceding the Spanish Conquest. One of those civilizations produced Teotihuacán, a city so rich and impressive that the Aztecs, centuries later, were to call it "the abode of the gods."

THE EDITORS

ANCIENT MEXICO
IN HISTORY

I
The City of the Gods

From a distance the great pyramids of Teotihuacán are as dun-colored as the earth in which they are set, and their vast bulk seems deceptively diminished by the dry plateau that stretches boundlessly to the horizon. But on closer scrutiny, the illusion changes — it is not the Pyramid of the Sun nor the Pyramid of the Moon that seems small, but rather the people who clamber over them or who are swallowed up in the enormous Avenue of the Dead. This thoroughfare bisects what is probably the most important and surely the most mysterious ancient city in the entire New World.

The name of the city is pronounced tay-oh-tee-wah-KAHN, which in the Aztec language means "abode of the gods." It was already in ruins when Moctezuma was emperor of the Aztecs, and its history was little more than a skein of myth when Hernán Cortés, seeing the ruins in 1520, became their European discoverer. The Aztecs believed that Teotihuacán was built by a race of giants, a notion that must have seemed all the more plausible when the bones of mammoths were found in the same soil. Figuratively speaking, the builders of Teotihuacán were indeed giants, a race of innovators, because in this dusty valley where water is so precious, they somehow managed to create the first true metropolis in the Americas. We can now say with some confidence that the urban revolution in the Western Hemisphere had its beginning here, some thirty miles northeast of Mexico City, in a tableland where today one finds more lizards and clumps of cacti than people. The achievement was in every way remarkable, more so because the Teotihuacanos — their real name is lost — did it on their own; so far as we know, they had no connection with the Old World, where the earliest cities had been founded many millennia before. "A nation has passed away," wrote the nearly blind American historian William H. Prescott, "powerful, populous and well advanced in refinement, as attested by their monuments — but it perished without a name."

Only within the past decade have we become more fully aware of the epic scope of the human miracle that occurred in the Valley of Teotihuacán. The dead city was intensively exhumed by Mexican archaeologists in 1962–64 (when a new highway was also built to the site, for the convenience of tourists). Simultaneously, a team of North American scholars began mapping Teotihuacán, locating no less than 2,600 major structures spread over eight square miles. The sheer number of buildings was a surprise, but more startling still was the manner in which they were arranged. As urban pioneers, the Teotihuacanos apparently moved straight from grammar to graduate school — the earliest American city turned out to be a rigorously planned community with markets and apartment houses.

Like Washington, D.C., Teotihuacán was laid out in quadrants on a precise gridwork pattern (see map, page 55). Its master plan allowed for growth, and its ceremonial, official, and private buildings were linked by ruler-straight streets. It grew in spasms. In around 100 B.C., the valley contained a cluster of villages from which the city slowly took form. It had a population of about 45,000 by the end of the second century A.D., and then reached its astonishing peak in the fifth and sixth centuries. At its height, Teotihuacán had a minimum population of 75,000, a probable population of 125,000, and a possible population of more than 200,-000. It was thus more populous than the Athens of Pericles and covered a larger area than the Rome of the Caesars. And then, having sprung seemingly from nowhere, Teotihuacán just as mysteriously collapsed, its buildings blackened by a conflagration that swept the city in about A.D. 750, nearly eight centuries before the arrival of Cortés.

The first American city was not only large but, by contemporary standards, it was clearly a pleasant place to live. If the great ceremonial plazas were imposingly spacious, the city's dwelling compounds were on an intimate scale, most of them arrayed around an open patio in the atrium style of the Mediterranean. The exterior of the single-story apartment compounds was generally white and windowless, but within, the walls blazed with color, for like modern Mexicans the Teotihuacanos were superlative muralists. Instead of doors there were hanging curtains to assure privacy, and the layout of the more than two thousand compounds in the city engagingly suggests that there was someone very like a concierge to greet callers. Most of the dwelling complexes were of a standard size — about three hundred feet long — and apparently housed clans or professional guilds. Professor René Millon of the University of Rochester, the director of the Teotihuacán mapping project, was struck by the sophisticated amenities he found. "Each patio had its own drainage system," he reported. "Each admitted light and air to the surrounding apartments; each made it possible for the inhabitants to be out-of-doors yet alone. It may be that this architectural style contributed to Teotihuacán's permanence as a focus for urban life for more than five hundred years."

The typical Teotihuacán dwelling was a one-story building with a number of apartments looking out on patios, some of which contained small, raised temples. The walls were surfaced with plaster and decorated with brilliant frescoes. To protect these frescoes, the ruins have been partially covered with new roofs of modern building material.

Overleaf:

This panoramic view of Teotihuacán looks south from the Pyramid of the Moon with the Pyramid of the Sun at left. To the right is the two-mile-long Avenue of the Dead, flanked by mounds that once formed the bases for lesser temples.

There was nothing jerry-built about the apartment compounds, which were set on foundations of moisture-resistant concrete composed of crushed volcanic rock mixed with lime and earth. A network of wooden posts provided extra support for concrete roofs, while walls were made of either stone or mortar or packed adobe brick. According to Dr. Millon's careful calculations, in most dwellings there were an average of thirty rooms used solely for sleeping space. By conservatively assuming that there were at least sixty persons living in the typical compound, he was able to calculate the probable population of 125,000 at the city's peak. Yet curiously, from all the evidence this great city was not warlike — there was no encircling system of great walls, nor are military motifs predominant in the art of Teotihuacán. It was, more likely, the capital of a peaceable kingdom, a theocracy whose influence extended as far south as present-day Guatemala, where pottery of a Teotihuacano style has been found in classic Maya sites.

In this Pax Teotihuacana, diplomacy and trade were assuredly important, for there was even the equivalent of an embassy row in the ancient city. In the eastern part of Teotihuacán, North American archaeologists found a dense concentration of pottery in the styles of the Maya and the Zapotecs, the two great kindred powers of Mesoamerica. The alien pottery suggests that a foreign colony lived in this area. In addition to maize and other produce, the Teotihuacanos undoubtedly sold pottery and obsidian trinkets — just as Mexican children do to tourists today — to awed visitors to their great city. In the market areas, postholes have been found that evoke a picture of brilliant canopies, of stalls, of pleasurable haggling over the terms of trade.

But it was not only goods that changed hands. Just as unquestionably there was earnest discussion about religion, for the Indians lived (and still live) in a god-haunted cosmos.

The original names of the gods are lost, and their exactions can only be surmised. But the piety of Teotihuacán is indicated by the chronology of its construction — the two great pyramids were built in the early years of the city's expansion. The larger is the Pyramid of the Sun, a mountain of earth sheathed in adobe and stone, as high as a twenty-story building and covering seven hundred square feet at its base. A broad stairway, which seems interminable as you climb it, leads to a flat platform on which a temple or altar probably once stood. It is worth making the huffing ascent, for from the top of the Pyramid of the Sun one can see the plan of Teotihuacán imprinted in the brown earth.

Below is the broad Avenue of the Dead, more than two miles long and lined with ceremonial platforms. It runs in a north-south direction and is very much like the Mall that serves as a similar axis for Washington. To the north, the avenue empties into a large plaza in front of the Pyramid of the Moon (all the names were given by the Aztecs), which is smaller than its solar brother but still covers four hundred square feet at its base. Priestly dwellings are clustered around the pyramid. One of these, the Butterfly Palace, has been expertly restored by Mexican archaeologists. To the south, there is still more to see; a vast compound known as the Citadel, a parade ground fit for a Napoleon and large enough to hold two divisions. The marketplace of the ancient city is on one side of the Citadel, while underneath it was the earlier Temple of Quetzalcoatl,

After more than a millennium spent flat on its back in a dry streambed near the village of Coatlinchán, the statue of Tlaloc, the rain god, was moved to Mexico City in 1964 on a special trailer (right). The removal was accomplished over alarmed protests by local villagers, many of whom believed that were the god to be moved the rains would cease. They parted with their deity only on the promise of a road, a school, a clinic, and electrification — and have been reassured since then by all of these plus a rainfall that has not been abnormal.

a smaller structure famous for the plumed serpents protruding from its base — big, toothy creatures with flecks of green and red paint still visible. Whatever their other demands, the gods of Teotihuacán had a taste for the monumental.

This monumental solidity is also reflected in the plastic arts of the city — in the squat, three-legged vases, in the unsmiling funerary masks, and above all, in the colossal statuary of Teotihuacán. The single largest worked stone block in Mesoamerica is an enormous statue known as the Water Goddess. There is nothing feminine about her proportions, however; she is twenty-three feet high and fourteen feet wide. She was found in the Plaza of the Moon and is now in the National Museum of Anthropology in Mexico City. Fittingly, the museum has at its entrance still another monolithic statue carved by Teotihuacanos, a giant figure of Tlaloc, the rain god.

There is a charming story about how Tlaloc came to Chapultepec Park, where the new National Museum, one of the most splendid in the world, is located. For several thousand years Tlaloc had been lying horizontally in his original quarry near Texcoco, possibly because he was so big that his creators could not figure how to uproot him. When the National Museum was being completed in 1964, Mexican designers thought it would be appropriate to move the rain god from his stone bed to his present post at the portal. With some difficulty, Tlaloc was excavated from the quarry and hoisted onto a special truck with hundreds of rubber wheels. He was ceremoniously carried to Mexico City and thousands turned out to see his arrival — in a torrential downpour. It continued to rain that night,

though it was not the wet season. "People joked about the coincidence," writes the Mexican author Victor Alba, "but later, as Tlaloc was being set in place in the museum garden, rain poured down each time he was moved, and the Mexicans began to feel an astonishment not far from superstitious awe, a response they only partly concealed by jokes."

That awe, that embarrassed astonishment, felt by modern Mexicans has an honest and ancient pedigree. From the outset, the New World perplexed and impressed its discoverers if only because it was not supposed to exist. So certain was Columbus that he was in the East Indies that he called the primitive inhabitants he encountered Indians, thus commencing the confrontation between Old and New World on a proper note of confusion. In every respect — ethnographically, historically, and theologically — the Western Hemisphere was the moon's dark side to its first explorers. Its independent achievements simply could not be explained, and even today eminent scholars refuse to believe that the Indians of the Americas evolved high civilizations without outside aid and advice.

A very special problem was rooted in Christian theology. The great Florentine historian Francesco Guicciardini, writing in the 1530's, noted that the Columbian voyages had "given some cause for alarm to interpretors of the Holy Scriptures" because the Americas seemed to contradict the verses in the Psalms that declared that the sound of the songs had spread to the very edges of the world. This was taken to mean that knowledge of Christ had spread over the entire globe through the mouths of the Apostles — an interpretation contrary to truth, Guicciardini coolly remarked,

"because no knowledge of these lands had hitherto been brought to light, nor have any relics of our faith been found there." So touchy was this point that the passage was suppressed by censors in all the editions of Guicciardini's monumental *History of Italy* that appeared before 1774.

Yet we have reason to be grateful for this vexatious doctrinal question. In 1519, Hernán Cortés landed in Veracruz, and with a relative handful of soldiers — and with the indispensable help of the terrifying horse — he subdued most of Mexico within two years. The Indians whom Columbus saw were primitive to European eyes, but this was decidedly not the case in Mexico. There is almost an air of baffled surprise in the letter dated October 13, 1520, that Cortés sent to his emperor, Charles V, describing the marvels of the Aztec capital, Tenochititlán, on whose ruins Mexico City was to rise. The conqueror wrote: "Yet so as not to tire Your Highness with the description of the things of this city . . . I will say only that these people live almost like those in Spain, and in as much harmony and order as there, and considering that they are barbarous and so far from the knowledge of God . . . it is truly remarkable to see what they have achieved in all things."

Cortés was a hard-bitten soldier, not a scholar, but in the wake of his conquest came learned priests who took a serious interest in all things Indian. The Spanish churchmen wished to know about heathen ways in order to facilitate conversion, but they were also deeply concerned with Indian history, if only to find evidence that the Apostles had somehow reached the New World. Thus they attentively questioned the Indians and learned that the Aztecs had entered the Valley of

Mexico in the twelfth century A.D. — they had been preceded by another warrior people, the Toltecs, who had once ruled in a splendid capital called Tula. With some delight, the clerics also heard that the Toltecs had a famous and fair-faced king who had taken as his title the name of the venerable Mesoamerican god Quetzalcoatl, or "Feathered Serpent," and who had ruled wisely, teaching all the civilized arts, before he sailed away to the east, promising to return.

By one of history's more incredible coincidences, Cortés chanced to land during the year the Aztecs called One Reed, the very year in which it was prophesied that Quetzalcoatl would return. This coincidence was of inestimable use to the crafty Cortés, and the story was also helpful to the churchmen, because in their eyes the god-king could have been one of the Apostles. Before long it was seriously argued that the Indians were in truth the Lost Tribes of Israel; to the Dominican friar Diego Durán, writing in the 1580's, the Aztecs were manifestly Hebrews.

More wonders were to await the Spaniards. Following in the path opened by Cortés, other conquistadors pressed south and absorbed the Yucatán and present-day Guatemala into the Spanish realm. By 1697, the entire Maya area was under Castilian control, and here the Europeans encountered another brilliant Indian civilization — a tribal nation of superb builders and gifted artisans. Moreover, the Maya were literate and had evolved the only true form of writing native to the New World. Once again, the clerics took notes, recorded old myths, learned some of the secrets of the Maya script, and left us a body of information whose importance is incalculable.

Yet what the churchmen could hardly have guessed was that the history of pre-Columbian Mexico was richer, more intriguingly complicated, and vastly older than the boldest imaginings of the first European explorers. In truth, it is only within the last century — and most especially in the past three decades — that the breadth and depth of Indian antiquity has been bared to light. A comparison may be helpful. Imagine that Western Europe was discovered by strangers in the sixteenth century and by earnest questioning these voyagers learned of Charlemagne and the Roman Empire. But missing from the story would be the Greeks, the Egyptians, and the Sumerians. Until very recently, our knowledge of Mexico before Cortés was similarly truncated.

In the pages that follow, the larger story will be told, because without some knowledge of it the ruins of Teotihuacán are hardly comprehensible. In its essence, the theme is both inspiriting and minatory. If the history of the New World civilizations has a message, it is that the human race can overcome the most formidable obstacles, for in the New World parched land was made to bloom and impenetrable jungles, inhospitable to mortal existence, were tamed by builders of vast temples. And this was done without the help of iron tools, or of oxen and horses, or indeed without the wheel. Yet if the great Indian civilizations rose to impressive heights, they also, for still obscure reasons, fell; great cities were abandoned to chattering monkeys and dozing lizards.

There is a further reason for plunging into the Mexican past. Far more than the United States, Mexico is obsessed with its ancient roots. In the words of the Mexican poet Octavio Paz, "The history of Mexico is the history of a man seeking his parentage, his origins." With a touch of proud despair, Paz has described his country as a "labyrinth of solitude." To the visitor, the solitude is palpable in driving through endless stretches of sunburned earth, the highway bounded by solitary stalks of maguey and lonely adobe huts. One also feels it in the jungles of Chiapas, where a parrot's shriek resounds like a thunderclap — but one is also aware of it in Mexico City's gleaming subway, where even during rush hour the loudest sound is the purr of rubber wheels.

There is both justifiable pride and a certain brooding melancholy in the way in which Mexicans look backward to a magnificent past. The pride is obviously evident in the inscription, in Spanish, which greets visitors to the National Museum of Anthropology: "Valor and confidence to face the future is found by people in the grandeur of their past. Mexicans, look at yourself in the mirror of this splendor; stranger, know also the unity of human destiny. Civilizations pass, but man has always within him the glory of those who struggled to bring him into being."

But there is melancholy, too. In scrambling among the pyramids and in being herded into a tourist bus, the alien traveler in Teotihuacán may miss this dimension. The loss is his. Something of the unique flavor of Mexico will elude him, a fatalism as much a part of the country as its parched plateaus and snow-tipped mountains. There is, in the history of Mexico, a profound music, a poignant fugue, and one of its expressions is in the ruins of Teotihuacán. But the story, as with all proper stories, should begin in the beginning.

MUSEO NACIONAL DE ANTROPOLOGIA

II
In the Beginning

More than a century ago, a lively Scotswoman wrote one of the classic works on Mexico. Her name was Fanny Calderón de la Barca, and her book, *Life in Mexico,* was drawn from the long letters she sent to her family in Edinburgh. Señora Calderón was the wife of the first Spanish ambassador to independent Mexico, and from the moment of her arrival, in 1838, she showed a shrewd appreciation for the beguiling complexities of Mexican life. She was struck, for example, by the love of flowers she discerned everywhere:

> In the poorest village church the floor is strewed with flowers, and before the service begins fresh nosegays are brought in and arranged upon the altar. . . . We are told that in the days of Cortes a bouquet of rare flowers was the most valuable gift presented to the ambassadors who visited the court of Montezuma, and it presents a strange anomaly, this love of flowers having existed along with their sanguinary worship and barbarous sacrifices.

In due course, Fanny Calderón visited the great pyramids of Teotihuacán. She was properly impressed, but nearly everything she said about the dead city turned out to be wrong. She blamed Cortés for destroying the sanctuaries, when in fact the conqueror had nothing to do with their ruined state. She described Teotihuacán's spacious avenues as a great burial plain, "composed . . . of the dust of their ancient warriors, an Aztec or Toltec Père-la-Chaise." In truth, as we presently know, neither the Aztecs nor the Toltecs ever inhabited Teotihuacán, and the avenues could scarcely be like the famous Paris cemetery since few burials have been found in the city. Finally, Fanny Calderón, no doubt to impress her Scottish kinfolk, told of seeing fragments of obsidian knives "with which the priests opened the breasts of their human victims." The Teotihuacanos were a pacific people; there is no evidence that anything like mass human sacrifices was carried out by them. (No such sacrifices are depicted in any of the paintings found in Teotihuacán.)

Still, one can hardly blame the vivacious Fanny. Her errors illustrate not merely the lapses of contemporary knowledge, but also the proximate nature of our present-day information about the pre-Columbian past. Discoveries made only in the past few years have radically revised our picture of the ancient American world, and today's certitude can be undone by a chance find tomorrow. This is one of the fascinations of the subject; it is very much like an unfinished detective story in which new clues, appearing in embarrassing profusion, keep changing the plot.

It is still not clear, to cite an example, when the first men came to the New World. Scholarly estimates range from as early as 60,000 years ago to as recently as 10,000 B.C. On one point the evidence does seem conclusive. The first Americans were homo sapiens, members of our own species, because thus far no one has found the bones of such prehominids as Peking or Java man, or the Neanderthaloids. Nor have the remains of any higher primates been found anywhere in the New World. There is also agreement that the first Americans came from somewhere in Asia, entered the hemisphere by way of the Bering Strait, and were most probably nomadic hunters in pursuit of ice age game. On everything else there is generous room for dispute.

The last ice age was the Pleistocene (meaning "most recent") and it persisted for perhaps a million years,

covering large tracts of North and South America with glacial sheets. The final retreat of the glaciers did not occur until around 10,000 B.C., and during the late Pleistocene period the face of the Americas was totally different. Areas that are now deserts were then dotted with lakes and covered with foliage. Enormous mammals, including mammoths and mastodons, which were already extinct in the Old World, still survived in the New (a circumstance that caused a good deal of initial confusion in the attempt to date the arrival of the first Americans).

We can assert with some confidence that early hunters, armed with spears, stalked and killed this giant game; a favorite tactic was to trap the mammoths in shallow lakes and swamps, where the beasts might become mired. This has been confirmed by a number of finds on the shorelines of vanished lakes, such as the discoveries made in the 1930's on a desolate and wind-swept plain in eastern New Mexico. Archaeologists were led to the region by a preponderance of fossil animal bones and chipped-stone artifacts on surface sands. At a site called Blackwater Draw, near the town of Clovis, excavators uncovered a stratified layer containing bones of mammoths and shaped projectile points, or "Clovis points." The site was clearly a "kill" area in a location once filled with glacial ponds and lakes. Camel, horse, and bison bones were later found at Blackwater Draw, also in association with Clovis points. When did the great feast take place? Organic material in the earliest stratum was given a radiocarbon date of 9220 B.C., and it is considered one of the most solid dates we have for the first appearance of these earliest of Americans.

Other prehistoric sites, some in South America, have yielded far earlier dates, but their testimony is not quite as solid. In 1946, Dr. Willard F. Libby of the University of Chicago discovered that the radioactivity of carbon dwindles at a fixed and measurable rate, and provided an important tool to archaeologists. All organic material contains carbon, and in theory the carbon 14 test, as it is called, can be used to date anything organic with rough accuracy. But the catch is that the material tested may be an intrusion in the site, especially in cases where excavation is not rigorously controlled. Thus, two supposedly ancient charcoal hearths were found at Lewisville, in northeastern Texas, in apparent association with an abundance of animal remains and some man-made artifacts. The charcoal was dated to 36,000 B.C. But regrettably, earth-moving machines were used to excavate the site, and the artifacts could well have been dragged to a lower level and mingled with burnt vegetation.

Initially, there were similar doubts about an otherwise sensational discovery in the Valley of Mexico, not far from Teotihuacán. In 1947, Mexican archaeologists unearthed a human skeleton near the village of Tepexpan, on the edge of the old beds of Lake Texcoco, an area known for the abundance of its Pleistocene fossils. Tepexpan man appeared to be the oldest known Mexican, but when his discovery was announced, non-Mexican scholars spoke darkly about "irregularities" in the excavation. Irritated Mexican archaeologists then intensified their search, asking all local people to report any "giant bones." The effort was rewarded, in 1952–54, with the location of the remains of two imperial mammoths near the village of Santa Isabel Iztapán.

This time, the excavation techniques were meticulous, and the Mexican prehistorian Luis Aveleyra was able to convincingly demonstrate that the beast had been butchered on the spot by the contemporaries of Tepexpan man.

Tepexpan man, it turned out, was actually a woman, five feet seven inches tall, with a mesocephalic skull shape similar to that of present-day Mexicans. A charcoal hearth found next to the slaughtered mammoth yielded a carbon 14 date of 7710 B.C., plus or minus 400 years, and this date most probably applies to the human skeleton. Man or woman, the Tepexpan person was surely typical of the tens of thousands of nomads who pressed through the forests of the New World, ultimately settling most of the hemisphere. For these first Americans, geography was destiny. Mountains, deserts, and oceans imposed natural frontiers within which radically different cultures evolved. It is estimated that by 1492, the Indians of the Americas spoke some two thousand mutually unintelligible languages, most deriving from perhaps as few as six basic linguistic stocks. Adaptation to different environments contributed to what scholars called genetic drift, with the result that there is greater variation in physical type among American Indians than in the Caucasian peoples.

Equally striking was the range of cultural achievement. At one extreme, there were the Indians of Tierra del Fuego, whose brutal primitivism appalled Charles Darwin when he encountered the tribe in 1832 during his voyage on the *Beagle*. Living on the pitiless tip of South America, the Tierra del Fuegans were ignorant of fire, slept on wet ground, cultivated nothing, conversed in what sounded like growls, and showed a

SILIQVASTRVM TERTIVM   Langer Indianischer Pfeffer.
99

The European medieval diet, monotonous and drear, was first enlivened by spices from the Orient, then further enriched by new comestibles from the New World. Three of these additions, shown here, were illustrated in 1542 by Leonhard Fuchs, the German botanist for whom the fuchsia is named. The plants include a pumpkin (far left), a red pepper plant (left), and the first representation of corn by a European (below). As the label indicates, Fuchs apparently had the idea that corn was of Turkish, rather than American, origin.

murderous hostility to all strangers. They were Swiftian caricatures of the human race; Darwin said of them in a descriptive letter he wrote to his sister, "I feel quite a disgust at the very sound of the voices of these miserable savages."

At the other extreme there were the high Indian civilizations, whose artistic and political achievement was hardly miserable or savage. There are twin peaks on the cultural horizon, one of them in the Andean regions of South America, where the Incas were the rulers of an empire extending for some 2,500 miles, the heirs of a rich tradition reaching back many centuries before the birth of Christ. The other peak was in Mesoamerica. Here Indian peoples ascended still higher, creating at Teotihuacán the earliest American metropolis and inventing in the Maya areas a unique form of writing and computation. The heirs to this tradition were the Aztecs, a warrior people with a vibrant culture which, however ferocious, was clearly not mean.

How did these twin peaks arise, in apparent independence from each other, as well from the Old World? We have no answers, but we do have clues, and the most important of these concerns agriculture. Civilizations, like armies, advance on their stomachs. The first requirement for settled life is a dependable source of food. In South America, early farmers made an epochal discovery — the potato. A still more important innovation occurred in Mesoamerica; the descendants of nomadic hunters in some unknown way learned to cultivate maize, or corn.

Corn is a miracle crop. It is calculated that a family of three can grow in 120 days, and without irrigation, twice as much corn as it can consume in a year. By

TVRCICVM FRVMENTVM.
Türckisch korn.

The all-but-miraculous staples of early Mexican agriculture were celebrated in a variety of ways. The dog at left, bearing an ear of corn much as a modern dog might carry a newspaper, was clearly created by an artist in a cheerful mood. It could almost be carrying the corn to the woman with the metate at right for grinding into a tortilla. The figure at far right carries a squash, another early mainstay of the Mesoamerican diet.

contrast, a Chinese peasant growing rice needs far more effort to produce much less. The fecundity of corn gave the Indians of Mesoamerica the gift of time that could be used to create cities, build temples, and speculate about the cosmos.

In Mesoamerica, the magic of corn was fully appreciated. An Aztec myth relates that the god Quetzalcoatl, who created mankind with his own blood, changed himself into an ant in order to steal a single grain of maize, which the ants had hidden in a mountain. This grain was given to newly created man, much as Prometheus gave fire to the Greeks. Spanish friars also recorded this Aztec hymn:

> I am a tender Ear of Corn
> from your mountains I come to see you,
> I your god.
> My life will be renewed;
> the sapling man grows strong;
> he who commands in war is born!

Whatever else has changed, in Mexico today the staff of life is still corn. As in pre-Columbian times, corn is prepared by soaking it overnight in a solution of lime or ashes, to remove the unpalatable skin. The soaked kernels are then ground into meal with a stone rolling pin on a device shaped like a curved washboard known as a metate — of which a multitude of pre-Columbian specimens exist. Next, the ground meal is formed into the round, leathery pancake, the tortilla. As Fanny Calderón remarks of tortillas, "They have been used all through the country since the earliest ages of its history, without any change in the manner of baking them," though she adds, a trifle sharply, "They are considered particularly palatable with chili, to endure

which, in the quantities in which it is eaten here, it seems to me necessary to have a throat lined with tin."

But how did the cultivation of corn originate? The question is not as simple as it might appear, because corn is unlike other vegetables in one crucial respect — it cannot, because of its husks, reseed itself without human assistance. Confronted with this puzzle, botanists originally maintained that wild corn never existed, and that the ancestor of the present plant was almost certainly a hybrid product of cornlike wild grasses found in Mesoamerica. But inconveniently, fossil grains of corn pollen dating to at least 80,000 years ago were later discovered in test wells drilled in Mexico City, meaning that corn did exist long before man came to the New World.

The mystery has been resolved thanks to the joint efforts of a dissident botanist, Dr. Paul V. Mangelsdorf, and a gifted archaeologist, Dr. Richard ("Scotty") Mac-Neish. The botanist disputed the prevailing view that the ancestor of Indian maize was teosinte, a grass which resembles corn and is found in Guatemala and western Mexico. Through exhaustive research, Dr. Mangelsdorf was able to show that teosinte could not have been the ancestor of corn because it was in reality a hybrid product of already domesticated corn. The true ancestor of corn, he maintained, was a wild corn capable of dispersing its own seed.

In a parallel tour de force, MacNeish confirmed the botanist's deductions. Scotty MacNeish was a graduate student at the University of Chicago when, in 1945–46, he visited Mexico to gather information for a doctoral dissertation on the links between native Mexican cultures and those of the southeastern United States. By

chance, he visited the unusually dry state of Tamaulipas, on the Gulf of Mexico, just south of Texas. There he found mountain caves filled with organic remains preserved by the oven-hot air. It occurred to him that such caves might preserve the otherwise perishable evidence about the origins of agriculture, that within them he could find clues about the first domestication of the three staple crops of Mesoamerica — corn, beans, and squash.

MacNeish came back to the Tamaulipas cave in 1948, and in their desiccated floors found convincing evidence that by around 6500 B.C. the bottle gourd had already been domesticated by the hunters who sought shelter in the caves. He also found cobs of corn, dating to about 2500 B.C., which could have been cultivated, or which could have grown wild. The archaeologist came to believe that the Tamaulipas Indians, whatever their other virtues, were fairly conservative and without innovative skills, and that the cradle of agriculture was probably to be found farther south. After a field survey, he decided to look in the equally arid Tehuacán Valley, some 150 miles southeast of Mexico City.

His intuitive stroke met with dramatic confirmation. In January 1960, after a long, hot walk in the Tehuacán Valley, through thick growths of cactus and mesquite, he and two companions encountered a promising rock shelter whose floor was covered with goat dung. From this point, MacNeish's own words should be quoted, because no more important discovery has been made in American archaeology:

> Behind a large rock roughly in the center of the shelter we dug a two-meter square to a depth of about two meters, using trowels. We took out everything, in-cluding the loose dirt, by bucket loads and put it through a mesh screen to be sure that we missed nothing. Slowly we peeled off the successive strata.
>
> The uppermost layer yielded Post-Classic remains: the stratum underlying it contained Classic and a few Formative sherds: then there was a sterile layer. Underneath that was a thick layer which was obviously pre-ceramic. On January 27, after lunch, Pablo, working well down in the pre-ceramic stratum, recovered a tiny corncob no more than an inch long.
>
> Only half-believing, I took his place in the bottom of the pit. After a short period of troweling and cleaning away dirt with a paintbrush, I uncovered two more tiny cobs. We held in our hands possible ancestors of modern domesticated corn. The impression was confirmed a month or two later by Mangelsdorf when he examined the cobs at Harvard University. Still later the cobs were dated to 3610 B.C., plus or minus 250 years. . . . These were the oldest corncobs that had ever been found.

As Mangelsdorf had predicted, the earliest known corn had its tassel at the top of its ear and its kernels were not imprisoned by a husk, meaning that its seeds could be dispersed in a wild state. The earliest corn, in fact, more closely resembled grass than the vegetable we know today; it was only through centuries of cultivation that its cobs grew in size and that it came to be fully husked.

Following his exhilarating discovery, MacNeish directed a series of campaigns in the Tehuacán Valley. By the time the dig was completed, in 1964, MacNeish's team had uncovered the longest and most complete archaeological sequence so far discovered in the New

In the millennium preceding the Christian era, the craftsmen of the Valley of Mexico turned out a profusion of ceramic objects including bowls, vases, and pitchers. They also made figurines of various kinds, among which were dwarfs, dancers, and acrobats — perhaps reflecting the diversions and amusements of the festivals held to honor the gods. The terra-cotta contortionist at right is an example of this pottery, showing in its configuration the influence of the Olmecs.

World. The sequence extended from 10,000 B.C. to A.D. 1520, encompassing within it the beginnings of agriculture and of settled life. All together, 454 occupied sites had been located, and in major excavations at twelve of them, 140 stratified floors and occupational zones had been identified. The dig yielded about 10,000 artifacts, 500,000 potsherds and 50,000 ecofacts, or remnants of the environment. Among the ecofacts were dried human feces, whose contents could be analyzed, thus enabling Eric O. Callen of McGill University, in one of the eccentric specialties of archaeology, to identify the plants and animals consumed thousands of years ago.

As a consequence of the Tehuacán project, we now have what are in effect the identifiable rungs of an upward ladder. Even at the risk of inflicting on the reader a list of unpronounceable names, each rung deserves a few words if only to suggest the gradual and arduous rate of ascent.

The first rung, dating from 10,000 to 6700 B.C., is known as the Ajuereado phase, the name deriving, as in other cases, from a specific site. During these years, the inhabitants of the valley were grouped in nomadic families, or what MacNeish calls microbands. These bands moved camp three or four times a year, and in the winter hunting was probably the only means of subsistence. In other seasons, meat was supplemented with spring seeds or fall fruits. A variety of flaked stone tools were used, including scraper knives that suggest the working of hides.

In the next two phases — called El Riego and Coxcatlan and extending from 6700 B.C. to 3400 B.C. — the denizens of Tehuacán, by slow degrees, learned some of

the secrets of agriculture. Following the end of the Ice Age, the valley acquired something of its present appearance. As game like antelope and jackrabbit became increasingly scarce, the aborigines formed larger groups, or macrobands, and began increasingly to search for vegetable foods. At some point in the El Riego phase, some of the Indians hit upon the idea of planting seeds in the ground and returning to harvest the crop. Chili, avocados, and cotton are among the plants that appear to have been cultivated. In the Coxcatlan period, beginning about 5000 B.C., the inhabitants of Tehuacán discovered a form of wild corn with cobs no bigger than a cigarette filter. This was the decisive first stride to settled life.

A fourth rung, the Abejas phase, from 3400 to 2300 B.C., marked a period of consolidation. Larger permanent settlements begin to appear, some of them apparently occupied all year round. Dogs also make their appearance, along with cultivated beans and pumpkins. In the next phase — Purron, from 2300 to 1500 B.C.— there was another major innovation; for the first time, crude bits of pottery appear. The pottery, the earliest found in Mesoamerica, may have been copied from yet more ancient types still unfound elsewhere, but whatever the case, its development signifies another major stride.

By the time of the Ajalpan phase, from 1500 to 900 B.C., the Tehuacán Indians were full-time agriculturalists apparently living in wattle-and-daub villages with from one hundred to three hundred inhabitants. Their crops included hybrid corn, squashes, beans, gourds, zapotes, chilies, cotton, and avocados. Pottery was well made but unpainted, and figurines, many of

females, attest to a complex religious life and a possible matrilineal system of kinship. In the Santa Maria phase, from 900 to 200 B.C., there is the first evidence of irrigation and the rise of temple villages. This evolution continued in the succeeding Palo Blanco period, from 200 B.C. to A.D. 700, during which time villages were oriented to hilltop ceremonial centers with elaborate pyramids, plazas, and ball courts. The variety of food becomes still more abundant — tomatoes, peanuts, lima beans, guavas, and turkeys all make their appearance. Irrigation became a systematic practice. Lastly, there is the Venta Salada phase, from A.D. 700 to 1540, which saw the growth of commerce with other regions. Local exports included salt and cotton fabric. At this time, the Tehuacán Valley appears to have been divided into small kingdoms, each with its urban centers. And then, with the arrival of the Spaniards, the aboriginal sequence ends, to be supplanted by the cultural hybrid which constitutes Mexico today.

MacNeish and his associates would be the first to concede that their schematic sequence may be oversimplified, with the various phases subject to later modification. But the chronology they have painstakingly assembled is consistent with finds elsewhere and provides a useful overview. What may get lost in this dry recital of the various phases is the epic nature of the Indian achievement in the Tehuacán Valley and elsewhere in the Americas. Quite literally, everyone in the West pays unwitting tribute to the Indians each time he or she sits down at the dining table.

It takes a robust effort of imagination to picture the essential drabness of the European diet before the Columbian voyages. Before the discovery of the Americas, the Old World knew nothing of such staples as corn, potatoes, tomatoes, squash, or lima, kidney and navy beans (the poor man's protein). The rest of the world was equally ignorant of such vivifying commodities as vanilla and chocolate. Each of these crops was the product of centuries of laborious experimentation; the success of those experiments has made the New World a granary for humanity.

The first Europeans in the Americas were rightly impressed by Indian foods. One of the chronicles of the conquest of Mexico was written by a laconic soldier we know only as the Anonymous Conquistador. He was struck by the sumptuous menu served to Indian lords — "sauces and soups, cakes and pies of every kind of meat, fruits and vegetables, and fish which they have in abundance." This sturdy Castilian swiftly developed a love for the chocolate drink. He remarks that the Indians valued the cacao bean, from which chocolate is made, so highly that it was used as currency ("It is the most commonly used coin, but very unhandy after gold and silver"). He says of chocolate that it is "the most wholesome and substantial of any food or beverage in the world, because whoever drinks a cup of this liquor can go through the day without taking anything else even if he is on a journey."

A yet more fulsome testimonial to chocolate was offered by a later European visitor — a quirky Englishman named Thomas Gage, who traveled as a Dominican friar in Mexico and Guatemala between 1625 and 1637 (and who later turned violently against Roman Catholicism). Gage drank chocolate morning, noon, and night for twelve years, and he remarks, "And if by chance I did neglect any of these accustomed hours, I presently

Pottery figures served various purposes in ancient Mexico. The fish-shaped vessel at far left is partly utilitarian, partly exuberance, but the figures at center are probably funerary — intended to accompany the dead — as is the "pretty lady" above. The significance of the two bizarre figures at left is disputed, but they probably had some philosophical meaning that has not as yet been deciphered.

found my stomach fainty." He did admit that some persons who consumed too much chocolate "grow fat and corpulent by it" but in his case he found it a sovereign safeguard against obstructions, oppilations, ague, and fever.

Gage's account of his travels was published in 1648, and in its pages one can sense something of the impact of the Americas on the European imagination. Yet far more than New World food excited the Old World. Indian art caused an even greater sensation. On December 9, 1519, the first treasure ship from Mexico arrived in Seville, and in her hold was a collection of Indian ornaments sent by Cortés to Charles V of Spain. The king was so impressed that he arranged for an exhibition of the trove in Ghent, his birthplace, and in Brussels. Among those who saw the Mexican treasure was Albrecht Dürer, who wrote of them in his diary: "I have seen the things which were brought to the King from the new *golden land* . . . a sun entirely of gold, a whole fathom broad; likewise a moon entirely of silver, equally large . . . also two chambers full of all sorts of weapons, armor and other wondrous arms, all of which is fairer to see than marvels . . . I saw among them amazing artistic objects that I have been astonished at the subtle *ingenia* of these people in these distant lands. Indeed I cannot say enough about the things which were before me. . . ."

Scotty MacNeish's effort to find the source of Mesoamerican agricultural genius has its counterpart in the efforts of others to find the no less elusive source of the Indian artistic tradition. One of the pioneer archaeological detectives was the great Mexican artist, Miguel Covarrubias, about whom a few words must be

said. Born in Mexico City in 1904, Covarrubias acquired his first fame as a cartoonist in New York during the 1920's: his caricatures in *The New Yorker* and *Vanity Fair* remain one of the prisms through which we see the Jazz Decade. In the 1930's, the artist returned to Mexico and became absorbed in pre-Columbian art — so much so that he won a new reputation, as an archaeologist. At the time of his death, in 1957, Covarrubias was counted as one of the dozen or so leading interpreters of the Mexican past. His restless curiosity led him to exotic places — including the great pits of the brickyards around Mexico City.

From time to time, brickworkers came upon ancient burials filled with broken pottery and bits of jade, which they would then sell to collectors. One such brickyard, only twenty minutes by car from the center of Mexico City, was at a location with the Indian name Tlatilco, which means "Where Things Are Hidden." Here workers struck a rich vein of Indian archaeology — their finds including sensational figurines carved from dark green serpentine. As Covarrubias writes: "Tlatilco has become famous, not only among archaeologists but also among dealers and collectors; the prices skyrocketed a hundredfold, and making bricks became secondary to treasure-hunting before the feverish digging could be brought under control and systematic excavations begun."

The devastation wrought at Tlatilco is one of the tragedies in pre-Columbian archaeology. Since the 1940's, when the first finds were made, the artifact-rich brickyard has been wantonly pillaged, and hundreds of burials have been obliterated in a greedy quest for "objects." Still, some scientific work has been possible,

and Covarrubias himself directed a series of campaigns
at the site. As a result, a unique window was opened
into the origins of art in the Valley of Mexico.

Tlatilco was settled around 800 B.C., and it developed into a village covering some 160 acres; it is thus
squarely within the period that archaeologists call
Formative. In the 340 burials unearthed by archaeologists at the site, there were innumerable lavish offerings that conveyed the way of life during the Formative
period. On the pottery there were vivid depictions
of local fauna — armadillos, opossums, turkeys, bears,
frogs, rabbits, turtles, ducks, and fishes. Other portraits
showed acrobats, children carrying dogs, dancers wearing leg rattles, and couples on couches. Some of the art
showed a perverse delight in physical monstrosities —
deformed hunchbacks, double-headed persons, or faces
with three eyes. Still more unsettling, in the view of
Dr. Michael D. Coe of Yale, were clay masks split into
two distinct faces, one half a skull and the other an
idiot with a protruding tongue.

A sophisticated, if sometimes macabre, artistic tradition already flourished around 800 B.C., but what
were its origins? The finds at Tlatilco gave only an
oblique clue. In the Formative period, the burials already included objects made by another culture, a culture with an even more advanced artistic tradition.
Covarrubias, in examining the evidence, decided that
artists and magicians from this foreign culture formed
an elite at Tlatilco, perhaps even dominating the village as colonial masters. And who were the strangers?
To Covarrubias, the answer was clear — they were
probably Olmecs, the most mysterious ancient people
in Mesoamerica.

III
The Jaguar's Children

A skein of accidents led to the discovery of the Olmecs, the Promethean people whose achievements made possible the birth of Teotihuacán. In 1862, the Mexican scholar José Maria Melgar y Serrano was visiting a hacienda on the slopes of the Tuxtla Volcano in southern Veracruz. Sugarcane workers told him they had discovered a huge inverted "kettle" buried in the soil, which, when unearthed, turned out to be an enormous head. Melgar investigated and found a ten-ton head carved in volcanic basalt. The head had what looked to him like "Ethiopic" features. This led him to conclude that Africans had once been in Mexico, and he so reported in a brief notice of his find that appeared in 1868 in the bulletin of the Mexican Society of Geography.

José Melgar y Serrano had in fact encountered an Olmec head, now known as the Colossal Head of Hueyapan, but his report attracted little attention: strange things are always turning up in Mexican soil. However, another scholar, Alfredo Chavero, was struck by the similarity of style between the head and a large jade ax with a jaguar mask carved upon it that had been found. In 1883, Chavero published a picture of the curious ax, mentioning its unknown pedigree; again, the report escaped notice. A few decades later, in 1909, a dam was being built in the mountains of northeastern Puebla; while a mound was being leveled by hydraulic pressure, a North American engineer spotted a tiny object gleaming in the mud. It was the carved image of a jaguar. The engineer took the jade figurine with him to his home in San Antonio, Texas — it was so exotic he thought it was Chinese. When the engineer died in 1932, his widow sold the jaguar to the

American Museum of Natural History in New York, where the small carving came under the curious gaze of George C. Vaillant, the distinguished curator of Mexican archaeology.

Vaillant was fascinated by the piece — he put it in a drawer, and for several weeks he would take it out nearly every day to admire it. In an article published in 1932, the archaeologist maintained there was a kinship between the tiger face on the jade and the "baby faces" seen on carvings found elsewhere in Mexico. The style was not like that of any known Mesoamerican people. Vaillant speculated that it could have been made by a people called the Olmec, who were described in Aztec traditions as a highly civilized tribe living on the Gulf Coast and were famed for jade work. The Olmecs, he wrote, "move like shadows across the pages of Mexican history; a few notices that there were such people, a few delineations of a physical type foreign to the racial features of the known people like the Maya, and a handful of sculptures out of the known artistic traditions comprise the testimony of their existence." Perhaps, he ventured, investigations in the Olmec area might reveal the origins of the great theocracies of ancient Mesoamerica.

Vaillant's deductive feat can be likened to that of an astronomer who predicts the existence of an unknown planet through its gravitational pull on the orbits of known planets. The feat has its archaeological parallel in the Old World, where a handful of finds in Iraq in the 1870's ultimately led to the discovery of the Sumerians, the world's oldest civilization. The full measure of Sumerian achievement was confirmed in an epochal series of campaigns at Ur directed by Sir Charles Leonard Woolley from 1922 to 1934. That Englishman's New World counterpart is Matthew W. Stirling, the director of the Bureau of Ethnology at the Smithsonian Institution in Washington, D.C.

As early as 1918, when Stirling was still a student at the University of California, he became intrigued by a photograph of a "crying-baby" mask found in Mexico. The mask was in the Berlin Museum, and during a trip to Germany a few years later Stirling went to examine it and found its blue jade gleam even more entrancing than he expected. As in Vaillant's case, a single specimen converted Stirling into an enthusiast. After he joined the Smithsonian, the young scholar combed museum cases and archaeological monographs for further evidence, much of which led to the steamy jungles of Veracruz. In 1938, Stirling went to examine the colossal head José Melgar y Serrano had first discovered. It was at a site known as Tres Zapotes, and what struck Stirling in particular was that the great head was encircled by an abundance of mounds extending over an area of about two miles. He showed photographs of Tres Zapotes to the National Geographic Society, whose officers agreed to finance an expedition. Work began in 1938, and the initial excavations brought to light a multitude of sensational objects, including an inscribed tablet, known as Stela C, which had a date carved on it — the earliest date that had been deciphered on any monument thus far discovered in the New World.

The year could be determined because it was inscribed in the bar-and-dot numerical system used by the Maya, in which a bar denotes a five, a dot equals one, and a shell-like symbol stands for zero. According

The jadeite miniature mask at left shows its Olmec characteristics by its typically puffy face, flat nose, and large lips. Only three and a half inches high and not quite four inches wide, its purpose is somewhat enigmatic. The Olmec ceramic figure opposite combines an infant's physique with an adult's physiognomy.

to the most generally accepted formula for correlating the Western and Maya calendars, the year inscribed on Stela C was the equivalent of 31 B.C. — a full three centuries earlier than the oldest known Maya date. The announcement of the find, to put it gently, caused consternation. It undermined the tidy certitude that high civilization in Mesoamerica had originated in the Maya areas of the Yucatán Peninsula and in Central America. Along the Gulf Coast, the jungles are drenched in in-cessant rain (about 120 inches fall at Tres Zapotes an-nually); it was an improbable area for the origin of a civilization.

Stela C was only the first of a series of nasty shocks. While his work was still underway at Tres Zapotes, Stirling scouted another promising site, La Venta, about thirty miles to the south in the neighboring state of Tabasco. The La Venta complex had been dis-covered in 1925 by the Danish-born archaeologist Frans Blom and by Oliver La Farge, a lean, tanned New Yorker who later won a Pulitzer Prize for his novel, *Laughing Boy*. At La Venta, the two explorers had found a colossal head, which they erroneously ascribed to the Maya. To Stirling it was clearly Olmec, and in 1940 he began digging in La Venta, a swamp-locked "island" near the Gulf Coast. He uncovered what is still the greatest of all Olmec sites, a complex ceremonial center with an imposing pyramid, temple platforms, plazas, huge carvings, and tombs filled with exquisite jade.

The pyramid was made of clay, a squat structure 110 feet high and 240 by 420 feet at the base. According to the calculations of the California archaeologist Robert Heizer, a later excavator at La Venta, the pyramid must

have taken some 800,000 man-days to build. The carved stones testified to further prodigies. Stirling found four colossal heads, a fourteen-foot high stela weighing about fifty tons, and a number of huge altars. One of these was the Quintuplet Altar, so called because of the five enigmatic personages carved upon it. The mystery is that hardly any stone is found near La Venta or Tres Zapotes. Archaeologists surmise that the basalt boul-ders were quarried in the Tuxtla Volcano, about a hundred miles from La Venta. The stones were ap-parently dragged by sledges and floated on rafts, and human likenesses were then carved in the tough basalt. However, the Olmecs had no draft animals, nor did they have any metal tools.

In the opinion of the eminent Mexican scholar Ig-nacio Bernal, "The Olmecs were not only the first and finest sculptors of Mexico; they were also the first to work jade and indubitably were the greatest in this medium. No other pre-Hispanic people were capable of producing the infinity of jade objects with the mas-tery of the Olmecs." Tiny figurines, striking funerary masks, axheads, jewelry — all were produced by the thousands by the Olmec craftsmen.

But this poses another mystery. The jade employed by the Olmecs is technically known as jadeite, a min-eral superior to the nephrite variety of jade used in an-cient China — of the two stones, jadeite is harder, brighter, and acquires more luster after polishing. It is also rarer. One source of Mesoamerican jadeite has been located — an area in eastern Guatemala where the Maya and Olmecs found apple-green jade. But the Ol-mecs especially prized a nearly translucent blue-green jade of uncanny beauty, and the source of this stone

At right is the famous Stela C, recording the date interpreted as September 2, 31 B.C. At left is The Wrestler, *considered one of the finest extant pieces of Olmec statuary and dating from somewhere between the twelfth and sixth centuries B.C. Some think it may represent a ballplayer and its realism has caused speculation that it may have been an image of an actual person.*

has not yet been found. Somehow the Olmecs located this elusive gem and, with a bland disregard for the difficulties involved, worked the obdurate material in a variety of ways, in Stirling's words, "as though it were plastic."

As a result of Stirling's campaigns, which ended in 1946, the Olmecs were revealed as the master creators of a distinctive civilization that anticipated and influenced all its successors down to the Aztecs. But who were the Olmecs? When did they flourish, how did they live, and what brought their world to an end? Each question is seeded with land mines, around which scholars walk with caution. As Miguel Covarrubias wryly observed, the Olmec "problem" has grown so complex "that it is just short of incomprehensible even to most archaeologists, who handle it with the repugnance with which they would handle a rattle snake."

The name itself is highly misleading. When, in his 1932 article, George Vaillant spoke of the shadowy Olmecs he had in mind the mysterious tribe whose name means "Rubber People," whom the Aztecs described as ruling the Gulf Coast at the time of Cortés. But the archaeological Olmecs were obviously a far more ancient culture, and we have no idea what they called themselves. For want of a better term, "Olmec" has stuck with adhesive persistence. And when did they live? Following Stirling's discovery of Stela C, with its apparent date of 31 B.C., leading Mayanists were incredulous. One of them, the great English scholar J. Eric Thompson, published a paper drily entitled, "Dating of Certain Inscriptions of Non-Maya Origin," proving with recondite reasoning that the date on Stela C was a delusion.

Thompson's paper was so persuasive and his authority so great that for a while his arguments tipped the scales. Stirling and Vaillant were in the minority, along with Miguel Covarrubias and other Mexican scholars, in contending that the Olmecs predated the Maya. Ultimately the dispute was resolved with the advent of radiocarbon dating. A series of carbon 14 tests in the 1950's showed that the monuments of La Venta dated from 800 to 400 B.C., confirming that the Olmecs were indeed the predecessors of the Classic Maya. Improbable or not, the Gulf Coast appeared to be the cradle of Mesoamerican civilization, the birthplace of monumental architecture, writing, and the principal gods of ancient Mexico.

There is not a scrap of written history that can be read, aside from isolated dates such as those inscribed on Stela C. Some hieroglyphic texts have turned up, but the symbols have little in common with Maya glyphs. There is, for example, a short text on the Tuxtla Statuette, an amiable duck-billed godlet carved in jade and now a prize exhibit at the Smithsonian Institution. But the godlet is nameless and inscrutable. All that we know of the Olmecs is based on the testimony of art and archaeology. These voices, however elusive they are, do tell us something.

What did the Olmecs look like? The seemingly Negroid features on the colossal heads caused José Melgar y Serrano to contend that Africans had reached Mesoamerica, and others have made the same argument. In fact, the features represent an idealized form of facial types still to be seen among Indians on the Isthmus of Tehuantepec, the neck of jungle and brush in southern Mexico where some Olmec sites are located. More-

over, there is a variety of facial types in Olmec art, including bearded faces with aquiline noses. On the enormous Stela 3 at La Venta, Stirling encountered a bearded personage with a long nose, who was promptly nicknamed "Uncle Sam."

The symbolic nature of Olmec art defeats attempts at literal-minded analysis because through so much of the sculpture there runs an obsessive interest in a single fearsome animal — the jaguar. Even today Mexican Indians refer to *the* jaguar, with a respectful article, as if the great cat was a species apart. Early Spanish friars reported that Indians believed the jaguar could hypnotize its victims with its hiccups and that a hunter knew if he encountered a jaguar in the jungle he could shoot only four arrows — should the Indian miss on the fourth shot, the jaguar would leap with a vicious snarl and devour him. In pre-Hispanic cultures, the jaguar was a god of darkness and the hidden recesses of the earth — the animal was believed to cause eclipses by swallowing the sun.

Among the Maya, the spotted cat was called *uotan,* or "innermost," and in the Valley of Mexico it was known as *tepeyollotl,* or "heart of the mountain." Even after the Spaniards converted a Zapotec king to Christianity, the monarch continued to bring secret offerings to a special sanctuary consecrated to the Heart Jaguar in a great cave on a wooded island on the Tehuantepec Isthmus. Miguel Covarrubias quoted an ancient chronicle that described how pious friars countered the jaguar cult:

There was [Father Burgoa relates] among other altars one of the idol they called "Heart of the Land" which received great honor. The material was of great value, for it was an emerald [clear green jade] the size of a thick pepper pod upon which were engraved with the greatest skill a small bird and a little serpent ready to strike. The stone was so transparent it shone from within with the brightness of a flame. . . . The first missionary of Achiotlán [where the cave was located], Fray Benito, afterwards visited the sanctuary and succeeded in persuading the Indians to surrender the idol to him. He had it ground to powder, though a Spaniard had offered him three thousand ducats for it, and he poured the dust on the earth and trod upon it to destroy the heathen abomination and to show the impotence of the idol in the sight of all . . . .

In these stories one catches an echo of the jaguar worship of the Olmecs. The evidence suggests that the Olmecs believed that in the primordial era a woman had mated with a jaguar, giving birth to a race of werejaguars, in which human and animal features were mixed. Countless examples have been found of these werejaguars, invariably asexual and with the chubby features of a baby combined with gaping, snarling mouths. Apparently, the werejaguar was an early form of the Mesoamerican rain god, since the Aztec deity Tlaloc and the Maya god Chac are both depicted with scowling mouths. In depictions of other Olmec gods, there are comparable similarities with later deities. There is every reason to believe that the major gods of the Mesoamerican world acquired their early identity in Olmec lands.

Additionally, the Olmec social and political structure foreshadowed later patterns. A wealth of information about the Olmec way of life has emerged from the wet soil of a third major site, San Lorenzo, also in the trop-

La Venta was not a residence but a religious center and burial place for officials whose tombs (opposite) were filled with precious offerings. Other objects — not from La Venta — include the only extant Olmec wooden artifact, a ceremonial mask (above), a stone "baby face" (left), and a werejaguar (below).

The Olmecs' obsession with the jaguar is evident in their art forms — from clay figurines clad in jaguar skin (left) to symbolic patterns in mosaic. The mosaic floor at right, in the form of a highly stylized jaguar's face, was found buried at La Venta. It was a major prize unearthed by Matthew Stirling.

ical lowlands of southern Mexico, about midway between Tres Zapotes and La Venta. First explored by Stirling, San Lorenzo was excavated in 1966–68 by Michael D. Coe of Yale, who in his initial season exhumed charcoal samples in order to obtain radiocarbon dates. To Coe's surprise, the Olmec occupation of San Lorenzo dated from 1200 to 900 B.C., meaning that the settlement was several centuries older than even La Venta. The site was thoroughly mapped, and some two hundred small mounds were pinpointed — each bump of earth indicating that a family dwelling was once present. By estimating that five persons lived in each dwelling, Coe was able to calculate that San Lorenzo in its last years had a resident population of about one thousand persons.

An abundance of great stone carvings turned up — about sixty in all — but for Coe, the payoff came in March 1967 when, on the western side of San Lorenzo, he came upon an entire nest of buried stone figures, all of them mutilated. What was interesting was that the big sculptures had first been deliberately destroyed, and then respectfully buried. He writes of the find: "The amount of pent-up hatred and fury represented by this enormous act of destruction must have been awesome, indeed. These monuments are very large, and basalt is a very hard stone. Wherever possible, heads were smashed from bodies, 'altars' were smashed to pieces, and strange, dimpled depressions and slots were cut into Colossal Heads. . . . Why was this done? Because the Olmec monuments must have stood for the class of leaders that held the tributary populace in such a firm grip, forcing from them incredible expenditures of labor. These stones must have been the symbol of all

that had held them in thrall, and they destroyed these symbols with as much fervor as the Hungarian revolutionaries toppled the giant statue of Stalin in Budapest in 1956." But, Coe adds, the Indians must have feared the power of the carvings, because after being wrathfully assaulted, the statues were carefully buried. In this apparent internal revolt, we encounter an episode that was to be repeated elsewhere in pre-Hispanic Mesoamerica.

To Coe and other Olmec specialists, the evidence suggests that the first American civilization was dominated by civil lords rather than a priestly caste, though the rulers may also have had religious roles. One device that could have aided the masters of San Lorenzo was a polished concave mirror made of obsidian, which could ignite fires and cast a sunlike spot on dark forests. A more practical reason for the power of the elite was almost surely an understanding of hydraulic and agricultural technology. At San Lorenzo, excavators found a system of artificial lakes to assure a year-round supply of water, an elaborate drainage system (the earliest in the New World), and indications of levee corn farming. This last point warrants expansion because intensive corn farming may explain the early rise of San Lorenzo. The site is near the sluggish Coatzacoalcos River, which seasonally rises to cover the low-lying land with sheets of water. When the river recedes, it leaves a fertile deposit of mud and silt, much like the Nile in Egypt. As a result, *two* corn crops can be harvested each year at San Lorenzo, the first after the spring rains and the second after the floods have receded. Even today the river levees are considered prime land by local farmers, and those who wield political

The colossal basalt head below from San Lorenzo, the largest of some twenty Olmec heads thus far discovered, stands nearly ten feet high and weighs some twenty tons. The statue at right, also Olmec, that seems to resemble an ape may represent a mistake in the restoration. When the object was discovered, it lacked its entire lower face. The thick lips and protruding chin are a reconstruction.

control in villages are those who have control of the fecund riverbanks.

But the most startling aspect of early Olmec civilization is its ubiquity. Olmec art is found in an impressive geographic expanse — Olmec jade has turned up as far south as Costa Rica and El Salvador, and in Guatemala colossal heads showing Olmec influence have recently been found. The greatest concentrations of Olmec objects have appeared in the Valley of Mexico and in the southern states of Morelos and Guerrero, hundreds of miles from the Olmec heartland on the gulf. At a site called Chalcatzingo, on the eastern borders of Morelos, high in the mountains, a cluster of Olmec petroglyphs, or rock carvings, were discovered in 1934. They contain depictions of what seems to be an early form of the god Quetzalcoatl, the Feathered Serpent. Another sensational discovery was made in the unexplored mountains of southeastern Guerrero, where a painted cave was located at a place called Juxtlahuaca. The findings in the cave were reported in 1966 by Gillet Griffin of Princeton and Carlo Gay, an Italian-born devotee of Olmec art; in its penetralia is a unique polychrome representation of a bearded Olmec ruler wearing a feathered headdress and leggings of jaguar skin.

What were the Olmecs doing in Guerrero? The question is fraught with controversy. Miguel Covarrubias believed that Olmec civilization in fact originated in western Mexico, but his view is not accepted by most scholars. Clearly the Olmecs made their presence felt over an enormous terrain, probably sending colonists to settlements such as Tlatilco in the Valley of Mexico. But why? A persuasive theory favored by Michael Coe is that the ceaseless quest for jade and serpentine

impelled the Olmecs to open trade routes as far south as Costa Rica and as far west as Guerrero. In any event, by expanding through much of Mesoamerica the Olmecs anticipated the later expansion of successor civilizations, including the Teotihuacanos.

But one must be candid. Everything about the Olmecs remains open to dispute. The sagacious Covarrubias, writing in 1957, asserted: "Perhaps the most tantalizing problem in the study of Middle American art is that it seems to have no roots, no origins. The early cultures appear in full bloom, without the formative stages that would show a logical development from older, more primitive peoples on a pre-ceramic, pre-agricultural level." Some of the gaps have been filled. Thanks to the work of MacNeish, the origins of agriculture are now better understood. But the origins of Mesoamerican civilization still remain largely clouded in doubt.

In the absence of evidence, some authorities insist that Mesoamerican civilization was a transplant, the result of chance contacts with the Old World, either from Asia or the ancient Middle East. To prove that transatlantic contacts could have occurred, the Norwegian explorer Thor Heyerdahl in 1970 completed an Atlantic crossing on *Ra II*, a raft of papyrus reeds built by the Aymara Indians from Lake Titicaca in the Andes. Heyerdahl's feat did not, of course, prove that such a crossing *did* take place in Olmec times, only that it *could* have occurred.

In Ecuador, what appears to be solid evidence of a transpacific sea voyage has been unearthed at a site called Valdivia, excavated by Clifford Evans and his wife, Betty Meggars, both of the Smithsonian Institu-

tion. At a level which could be dated to around 3200 B.C., incised pottery without any known archaeological pedigree was found at the coastal site. The style of the pottery was strikingly similar to ware produced in the same period on the Japanese island of Kyushu, at the far edge of the Pacific, a place from which favorable winds and tides might send a stray fishing vessel across the sea. No such scientifically excavated evidence for transpacific or transatlantic contacts has yet been found in Mesoamerica, though Covarrubias, for one, believed that such cross-fertilization was possible.

The Olmec enigma persists. We simply do not know why or how an advanced civilization, without evident roots, suddenly flowered in the dense, humid jungles of the Gulf Coast. We do know that it happened, and there are some tantalizing clues — only wisps — as to the true identity of the Olmecs. Michael Coe has spotted one of them. An old poem, recorded after the Spanish Conquest and in the Nahuatl tongue of the Aztecs, speaks of a legendary land known as Tamoanchán, on the eastern shores, founded long before the rise of Teotihuacán:

> in a certain era
> which no one can reckon
> which no one can remember,
> there was at Tamoanchán
> . . . a government for a long time.

In this place, the Aztecs said, there were wise old men who had in their possession all the "writings, the books, and paintings." One day these sages left Tamoanchán, taking the books and the images of their gods with them. The people were in despair, but four wise men stayed behind and urged them to carry forward the

This grouping, unique in Olmec art, was found buried at La Venta and has been dated between 850 and 450 B.C. Just what it represents is uncertain. Figures of jade and serpentine confront a single individual of coarse stone whose back is to a wall made of jade celts. It might be a priest addressing a crowd or a prisoner about to be executed, but in any event, the juxtaposition of light and dark and the placement of the figures give it a real sense of visual drama.

light of civilization. These philosophers gave the people "the book of the days, the book of the years, the count of the years, the book of dreams. . . ." The saga continues: "And they departed from Tamoanchán. Offerings were made at a place called Teotihuacán. And there all the people raised pyramids for the sun and for the moon."

The Aztec legend is instructive in two respects. First, there is the name Tamoanchán, which makes no sense in Nahuatl. In the Mayan language, however, the term has a double meaning — both as "the Land of the Bird-Snake," or Feathered Serpent, and as "the Land of the Rainy Sky." If the name is Mayan, one gets a clue to the identity of the Olmecs. Linguistic studies have established that an isolated enclave of Mayan-speaking peoples exists on the northern Gulf Coast, in the states of Tamaulipas, northern Veracruz, and San Luis Potosí. In pre-Hispanic times, these isolated Mayan-speaking areas must have been contiguous with the Maya heartland to the south; the accidents of conquest cut off one Maya area from another. If so, there was once a continuous strip of Mayan-speaking areas from the Yucatán Peninsula to the northern Gulf Coast — and if so, the Olmecs were most probably a Mayan-speaking people. From behind the mask, the elusive Olmecs emerged as the Maya.

All this is speculation. What is clear is that the torch of civilization *was* passed, both to the Teotihuacanos in the Valley of Mexico and to other Classic civilizations to the south. The pyramid of La Venta may have spawned even greater monuments at Teotihuacán, in which case the connective strands of Mesoamerican culture form a seamless whole.

We do know that the high Indian civilizations in Mesoamerica were vitally interrelated, sharing common attitudes, observing a similar calendar, and worshiping many of the same gods. The kinship is best suggested by the image of the banyan tree of the tropics, whose branches fuse and cross, sending down adventitious aerial roots that evolve into supporting trunks. Outwardly, the banyan tree resembles a miniature jungle, but all its tangled branches are ultimately traceable to a parent root. It was the banyan that Ralph Linton had in mind when that eminent Yale anthropologist called his last book *The Tree of Culture* (1955), and his vivid imagery has been most gratefully borrowed here.

In Mesoamerica, the parent root was the Olmec civilization, and a hundred aerial branches grew from it, some reaching to the Valley of Mexico. The Olmec presence was evident at the site of Tlatilco, now a brickyard outside Mexico City. At the time of the birth of Christ, other settlements also emerged in the central highlands of Mexico; a notable one was at Cuicuilco, a site on the fringes of the modern capital, now within view of the imposing national university. Here Preclassic peoples erected a great adobe mound, an oval-shaped pyramid some 369 feet in diameter and about 60 feet high, with twin ramps leading to the summit. Cuicuilco is on the slopes of a volcanic range, and its pyramid seems to mimic the dread form of the active volcano. The volcanoes were very much alive, and an ancient eruption finally engulfed the site with soot-black lava as the terrified inhabitants fled. Radiocarbon dating has established that the eruption occurred around 100 B.C., confirm-

ing that the Cuicuilco pyramid is the oldest monumental structure in Mexico City.

A third early settlement was at Cholula in the Valley of Puebla, today an attractive city filled with hundreds of small churches with domes of glinting tile, over which an enormous pre-Columbian pyramid looms. George Vaillant evokes the atmosphere: "The people themselves are very Indian, and the strange sounds of Nahuatl often break in on the smooth syllables of Spanish. The big temple of Cholula is incredible. It seems like the counterpart of Babel, to which the friars compared it. On top a church rests proudly, and on a terrace below are the remains of rooms and the altar enclosing human burials, all carefully excavated by government archaeologists. Within the big mound run more than a mile of tunnels, which archaeologists hollowed from the adobe brick to follow the walls and stairs of the ceremonial precinct of earlier times. Deep inside, frescoed representations of the Butterfly God are awe-inspiring in the dim lantern light."

Built over a period of several centuries, the Great Pyramid of Cholula is some 180 feet high and extends over an area of 42 acres, making it, in terms of volume, the largest pre-Columbian structure in the New World. The origins of the mound reach into Preclassic times, but the precise chronology of the Cholula pyramid has not yet been established, and it is a prime target for further investigation.

What is apparent is that the Olmec tradition of temple building took seed in the central highlands, and that in one place — Teotihuacán — a great metropolis came into being around two vast pyramids. The first settlement at Teotihuacán can be dated to around A.D. 30, plus or minus 80 years, this being the carbon 14 date of charcoal found in the interior of an early mound. In the course of mapping the vast site, René Millon of the University of Rochester was able to clarify some chronological puzzles. The earliest pottery style in Teotihuacán belongs to what scholars call the Tzacualli phase. Tzacualli ware is in a polychrome style absent in later, datable periods of Teotihuacán, and thus its presence can be taken as evidence of early occupation. Before Millon began his research in the 1950's, the consensus among archaeologists was that the Tzacualli phase long predated the building of the great monuments. Millon found that complex structures were already being raised during Tzacualli times, or in the period known as Teotihuacán I.

In 1957, he and a colleague made an exploratory survey in a region north of the Pyramid of the Moon, hoping to discover refuse heaps which might contain Tzacualli pottery. What they actually found was a major extension of the building zone itself. He reported in 1960: "This was unexpected, mainly because we could not suspect that such a major building zone could have gone unnoticed or unappreciated. We found scores of mounds, none of great size, in a broad area about a mile long to the northwest and west of the Pyramid of the Moon. Some of the mounds are arranged in plazas, several of which are of great size." Teotihuacán, Millon concluded, must have been a city of tremendous size far earlier than previously guessed — even during Tzacualli times, in the first century A.D., it was apparently a sacred pilgrimage city with thousands of inhabitants.

"Downtown" Teotihuacán has been plotted by a team under the direction of René Millon. The gray area shows the main religious focus of the city — running from the Pyramid of the Moon (top) down the Avenue of the Dead, passing the Pyramid of the Sun (center), and terminating at the entrances of the Great Compound (bottom, left) and Temple of Quetzalcoatl (bottom, right). Stretching around this central core are as yet mostly unexcavated buildings, including dwellings.

During the city's ensuing Classic periods, known as Teotihuacán II and III, buildings of every sort began to fill an expanse of about seven square miles. Millon's belief is that the two great pyramids were erected during the Early Classical period, or Teotihuacán II, though a small interior platform within the Pyramid of the Sun appears to date from the Tzacualli phase. By A.D. 500, in his view, the city reached its zenith, with a probable population of 125,000 and a possible population of more than 200,000. Of these inhabitants, most were farmers, but Millon estimates that perhaps 25 per cent of the Teotihuacanos were involved in craft production and craft activities, suggesting a sophisticated division of labor that was far removed from the primitive slash-and-burn agricultural economy of early villages.

How can one explain the sudden emergence of so large a city? An obvious factor was Teotihuacán's strategic location on the best route between the Valley of Mexico and the Valley of Puebla, which in turn opens onto the lowlands of the Gulf Coast. A second possible reason is ecological — the Teotihuacán Valley is a rich, alluvial plain watered by hidden springs. While Millon was mapping the site, a team of scholars directed by William T. Sanders of Pennsylvania State University undertook a thorough study of the valley's ecology. As a result of the findings, Sanders believes that at an early period the Teotihuacanos used intensive farming techniques, terracing the slopes of the valley and irrigating them with flood waters. In his words: "The growth of the city, particularly in its early phases, was apparently related to the development of these techniques of intensive land-use." Yet the

hypothesis must be tentative, because there is no way of firmly dating the age of irrigation channels.

One contributing factor, surely, in Teotihuacán's rise was a gift of the volcano — obsidian. During his work at the Olmec site of San Lorenzo, Michael Coe was struck by the prevalence of obsidian implements, even though the black stone is not found in the Olmec heartland. A sampling of obsidian artifacts was taken, and each was ground into pellets for a chemical analysis of its components. It was thus possible to determine the source of the Olmec obsidian; some of it matched known sources as far away as Guatemala, and some originated in the Valley of Teotihuacán. On the eastern fringes of the valley, a particularly rich "staircase" formation of black obsidian is wedged between layers of red ash and lava.

Coe and his colleagues pointed out that the overwhelming majority of nonceramic objects found in Mesoamerican sites are made from the shiny black mineral. In a 1971 report, they noted: "The importance of obsidian for the economy of ancient Mesoamerican peoples was probably similar in magnitude to that of steel for the economies of modern industrial nations, for the Mesoamerican peoples manufactured most of their tools and weapons either from or with obsidian, and no doubt considered it a necessity for existence."

Millon has identified more than five hundred craft workshops in Teotihuacán. The vast majority of these were obsidian workshops, most of which were flourishing when the city was at its height.

It can also be sensibly surmised that the art of Teotihuacán was in lively demand in Classic Mesoamerica —

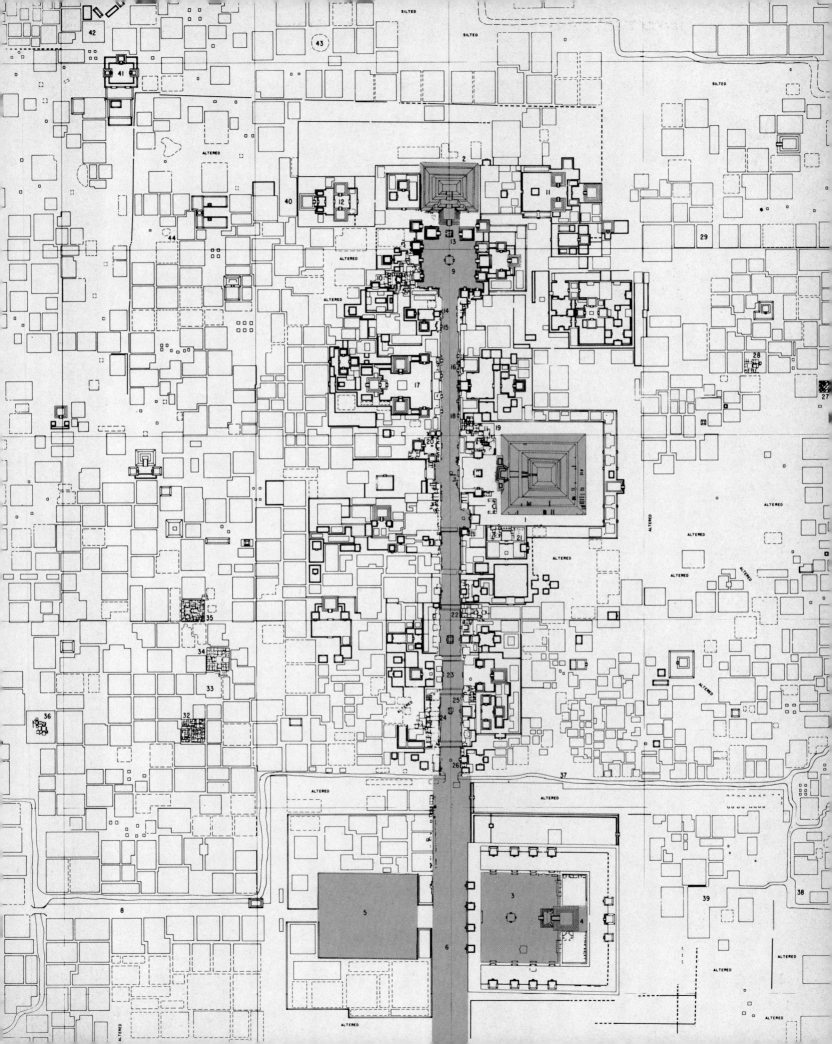

the city's wares have been unearthed as far south as Guatemala. The best description of Teotihuacano art is given by Miguel Covarrubias, who calls it "austere and distinguished, gay and graceful, and intensely religious." He continues: "It is clearly the product of a tight, disciplined elite, an intelligentsia of priest-rulers. Its principal subjects are the elements of nature: the waters and the mountains, trees, fruits and flowers, maize, cacao, butterflies, owls, and all sorts of birds; shells, snails, starfish, jaguars, coyotes, serpents, the spider monkey of the lowlands, armadillos, and so forth." The gods of Teotihuacán are omnipresent, with the snouted rain god Tlaloc predominating over the Feathered Serpent, the jaguar god, and the strange fire god, an old gnarled figure who carries a brazier on his head.

The pity is that so much Teotihuacano art has been churned up by illicit diggers searching only for what is salable and wrenching everything from its context. Covarrubias sadly points out that in more than sixty years of exploration at Teotihuacán, no important tombs have been found, though local treasure-hunters have sold to collectors fine objects that could have only come from tombs. Many of Teotihuacán's famous funerary masks have turned up on the market, but to date not one has been archaeologically excavated. Equally lamentable, the curious and precious wall paintings of Teotihuacán have been gouged from buildings and sold to collectors and museums.

But in any event, the surviving murals of Teotihuacán provide a unique glimpse into the life of the people who created them. In these paintings, one is struck by the absence of violent or martial themes, by their air of patterned cheerfulness, like wallpaper for a child's room. Another distinguishing trait is chaste asexuality. Not only men and women, but also animals are depicted without sexual organs. Caution is needed in deducing too much from artistic conventions; the art of Islam, it has been remarked, contains few depictions of the female body, but one cannot conclude on this basis that the adherents of Islam are uninterested in the female form. But taken with other hard evidence — such as the lack of elaborate fortifications at Teotihuacán — the murals clearly suggest a pacific way of life, a society that would seem to have been Apollonian rather than Dionysian.

Almost certainly the wall paintings contain a symbolic language that is lost or at best obscure. The Yale scholar George Kubler, who has made an intensive study of Teotihuacano iconography, has come to conclude: "The detailed meaning of the art of Teotihuacán remains a mystery. There are no texts coeval with its forms, and no image has been clearly or unequivocally identified in the terms intended by its maker." This absence of texts does not signify that the Teotihuacanos were illiterate; some inscriptions have been found on isolated works, and the presumption is that the city's engineers needed written archives to carry out building plans that extended over decades, even centuries. But whatever writing material was employed was perishable, and we are left only with the enigmatic symbols on paintings and pottery.

Attempts have been made to find a unitary key to the city's art. The French-born archaeologist Laurette Séjourné, who herself excavated a major palace complex at the site, sees in Teotihuacán art evidence of a

*Two details from wall frescoes at Teotihuacán show
Tlaloc (left), the rain god, with the water that gives life
to living things on earth springing from his hands and a
scroll issuing from his mouth that represents either
speech or song. The mythological birds (right) are part of
a painting from the Avenue of the Dead entitled* The
Animal Paradise.

conflict between the benign deities such as Quetzalcoatl and the later, bloodier gods of the Toltecs and
the Aztecs — but her theory is in dispute. Further research may provide a clue to the symbolic language.
An example of a fresh approach is the hypothesis ventured by a young Harvard architectural historian,
Stephen Tobriner, who himself worked at Teotihuacán in 1966.

In sifting through old documents, Tobriner was
struck by a passage in an official report made in 1580
to Philip II of Spain. The king had ordered a survey
of all his new territories in the Indies and had sent a
list of questions to be answered by his colonial officials.
The report on Teotihuacán — the earliest Western
reference to the ruin — contained a curious reply to a
request for information on "any remarkable and ad-
mirable works of nature there may be in the district."
The local official replied:

> Towards the north lies a big mountain which the
> natives name Tenan and it has given birth to many
> other mountains. On the eastern slope of the afore-
> said mountain, about half way up, is a chasm in which
> one hears a great noise which appears to proceed from
> the interior, at a distance of twenty yards. This seems
> to be the noise of the water which descends from said
> mountain. The natives are convinced that it is water,
> because in the whole of the plain between the town of
> San Juan [the Spanish name for Teotihuacán] and the
> confines of Texcoco there is no river nor springs other
> than the one at the head of the town of San Juan
> which the natives associate with the water which
> makes the noise in the mountain.

This reference fascinated Tobriner, and he learned

from a Harvard geologist, Professor Ulrich Peterson,
that volcanos collect water from rain that falls into
their silted-up cones; the water that cannot be absorbed
flows down the sides of the mountain, in streams under
the surface. That flow sets air in motion, which can
produce a noise. Tobriner also learned that the Indians
in Teotihuacán have for generations associated their
destiny with Tenan, which they call Cerro Gordo
("Fat Mountain"), the volcanic peak that rises behind
the Pyramid of the Moon. The entire plan of the
ancient city, with the Avenue of the Dead as its axis,
is aligned to the Pyramid of the Moon and to the Fat
Mountain behind it. In the studies of the valley's
ecology made by Sanders, the young Harvard scholar
found that the geographic characteristics of the area
had not changed in any major way for four thousand
years, and that the water for the area's present-day
irrigation system derives from eighty springs, all of
them concentrated in a single small region and linked
to Cerro Gordo.

In 1966, Tobriner climbed the Fat Mountain and
located in it a thin vertical shaft that emitted air and
noise of water traveling underground. He conjectured
that the Teotihuacanos believed that the mountain
was the source of the all-important water, and that they
associated the peak with worship of the rain god. Looking again at the paintings of Teotihuacán, he was impressed — as was Covarrubias before him — by the
plentitude of symbols suggesting mountains and water.
Here, conceivably, was a key to part of the visual sym-
bolism of the murals. The verdict is not in, but
Tobriner has at least looked at familiar evidence in an
innovative way.

The year 1962 saw the spectacular discovery of the richly decorated Butterfly Palace, near the Pyramid of the Moon. Its many rooms were embellished with frescoes and carved motifs, such as the eagle at left and the god Quetzalcoatl below. Glinting disks of obsidian often served as eyes (far left).

The evidence of archaeology is less ambiguous concerning the fall of Teotihuacán. In around A.D. 750, the city was sacked and burned, probably after an internal uprising (a likelihood suggested by the absence of alien artifacts that might have been left by an invader). A number of clues clearly point to a final conflagration. In 1962, a team of Mexican excavators directed by Dr. Jorge Acosta came upon a hitherto unknown palace complex near the Pyramid of the Moon. Now called the Butterfly Palace, the structure is a labyrinth of richly decorated rooms, the roofs of which were once supported by small wooden beams about five inches in diameter. The roof had collapsed, and the charred remains of the wooden beams were found on the stucco floor, giving the suggestion of some kind of holocaust.

But after the downfall of Teotihuacán, Classic civilizations continued to flourish elsewhere, among the Zapotecs in Oaxaca and the Maya in the Yucatán and upper Central America. One can imagine that runners brought the news of the catastrophe at Teotihuacán, an event which surely sent tremors through the entire Mesoamerican world. One can also guess that there were earnest debates about the news, and resolute declarations that it would "never happen here." But it did. By around 900, the Classic era was over and a dark time of troubles had begun.

As Teotihuacán fell, the principal Zapotec center — Monte Albán — was still one of the glories of pre-Columbian Mesoamerica; an immense complex of temples and plazas, including a ball court, an observatory, and hundreds of burial vaults. Like Teotihuacán, it was a painted city, and with its brilliant colors and

The luxury pottery of Teotihuacán was Thin Orange, made from a special clay that allowed potters to produce hard yet thin-walled objects in a pleasing shade of orange. Imaginative examples include vases such as a foot-shaped one above, a reclining figure at far right, and a dozing dog (below, center). Bowls ranged from the classic simplicity of the one at right to the jaguar-ornamented one below. The fragment below, far right, is adorned with an encircling band of clasped hands.

Between Teotihuacán to the northwest and the Maya centers to the southeast lay the Zapotec ceremonial city of Monte Albán (above). Its early, Olmec influence is shown in the stone **Danzante** figure at right dating from 500–200 B.C. The urn above, far right, dates from A.D. 600–1000, and the seated man at left falls chronologically between the two. This figure is a representation of a deity or a very important ruler, shown by the glyphs on his chest and headdress.

its hilltop setting, it must have seemed a surreal vision. Monte Albán is still an impressive ruin, dominating a man-leveled peak about six miles southwest of present-day Oaxaca. The climate is semitropical and the natural setting cinematic; the mauve and purple peaks of the Sierra Madre del Sur form a jagged backdrop to a city built mainly of lime-green stone. Visitors are quickly impressed by the charm and gregarious zeal of present-day Zapotecs, whose ancestors built Monte Albán. Immemorially the Zapotecs have been adroit traders and middlemen, serving as links between the central highlands and the Maya areas in the south. (Zapotecs have excelled as politicians; two famous Mexicans — the revered Benito Juárez and strongman Porfirio Díaz — had Zapotec blood.) The vast central plaza of Monte Albán, one guesses, was probably a marketplace.

The Olmec legacy is apparent at Monte Albán. In the period known as Monte Albán I, Preclassic figurines show a strong kinship to Olmec styles, and the linkage is clearly visible in the famous *Danzantes,* or "Dancers," a group of carved slabs that decorates the early buildings of Monte Albán. The carvings depict nude men — many hunchbacked, dwarfed, or club-footed — with curious stylized scrolls for sexual organs. Whether they are monsters, gods, or prisoners is not clear, but the telltale Olmec bar-and-dot glyphs appear on the same slabs. In the succeeding Classic era, or Monte Albán II and III, a distinctive art style appears. The rulers of Monte Albán favored elaborate burials, and tombs at the site have yielded a wealth of Classic era art — funerary urns, polychrome murals, jade masks, and fine cylindrical vases. For all its formal,

purely decorative quality, the art of Monte Albán reflects a sumptuousness, a love of display, that accords with the theatricality of the site itself.

Monte Albán was a place of pomp and pageantry, much more like a Maya ceremonial center than a complex metropolis like Teotihuacán. Although there are indications that some private residences did exist there, Monte Albán was primarily a seat of priests and kings and not a true city. But in around A.D. 900, the priests and kings together failed the people of Monte Albán, and the lofty site was abandoned, possibly as a result of attacks by aggressive newcomers in the Valley of Oaxaca, the warlike Mixtecs.

Even after its abandonment, however, Monte Albán continued to be a center of ritual and pilgrimage; the Mixtecs used it for royal burials, and the site was still known and revered when the Spaniards arrived. This was not the case at other Maya centers that were deserted at about the same time. There extinction was total, and even the memory of great sites was obliterated. All the sacred cities of the central Maya area were abandoned — Palenque, Tikal, and Copán — and the Maya virtually disappeared from the jungles they had vanquished, dispersing to such centers as Uxmal and Chichén Itzá in northern Yucatán and others in Guatemala that enjoyed a Postclassic revival and perpetuated Maya civilization until the Spanish Conquest.

Among the Maya, the Olmec impetus produced the most exuberant and mystifying of all Indian civilizations in the New World. The central area of Maya Classic civilization is a belt of some 800 square miles that runs through the base of the Yucatán thumb, reaching as far south as Honduras and north to the Mexican

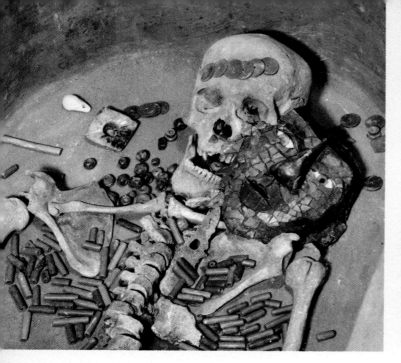

state of Chiapas. Much of this terrain is dense jungle, yet it was here that the Maya developed scores of impressive ceremonial centers, hit upon the mathematical concept of zero at least half a millennium before Europeans were awakened to the same useful discovery, developed a multiplicity of calendars, and not only calculated solar eclipse cycles but also computed the average lengths of the synodical revolutions of Venus. In Toynbee's terms, seldom has so oppressive a challenge met so vigorous a response.

Both the challenge and response are dramatically visible at Palenque, a site which takes its name from a nearby town in a remote corner of Chiapas. Because it is more difficult to reach than Maya sites in the Yucatán, fewer tourists visit Palenque, but those that manage the trip seldom forget it. From the village one takes a jeep that bumps down a dirt road into a thickening sea of foliage. Suddenly the city springs into view, resembling from the distance a toy ruin in a child's aquarium. An early explorer, the New York lawyer John Lloyd Stephens, described the initial impact of his visit in 1840: "Through openings in the trees we saw the front of a large building richly ornamented with stuccoed figures on the pilasters, curious and elegant, with trees growing close against it, their branches entering the door; in style and effect it was unique, extraordinary and mournfully beautiful."

The larger trees have been felled, but the panorama remains the same. Palenque's palace is a labyrinth coated with lichen, swarming with bats, and encrusted with carvings. It has an almost Italianate tower, much like a campanile. Its stucco sculpture shows Maya nobles, their noses hooked and their skulls flattened,

surrounded by courtiers sitting cross-legged. Around the palace are a number of small temples, each on a hummock of earth. Aside from the caretaker, there are no human inhabitants — Palenque is populated by hummingbirds, parrots, lizards, and howler monkeys, a natural zoo amid buildings of weird beauty, especially when seen at dawn, as the jungle quivers with life.

No one knows the true name of the city. First settled before the birth of Christ, Palenque reached its florescence between the seventh and tenth centuries A.D. Excavations have yielded tantalizing suggestions of its former prosperity and have caused a drastic revision in certain orthodox views about the Maya. From 1949–52, the Mexican archaeologist Dr. Alberto Ruz explored the Temple of the Inscriptions, a pyramid sixty-five feet high facing the palace. In a room on its peak, there are panels inscribed with 620 hieroglyphs, the dates covering a 200-year period — the date believed to be contemporary with the temple is A.D. 692. Ruz noticed that the floor of the chamber was covered by two large slabs, one of which had a double row of holes provided with removable stoppers. When the perforated slab was raised, a vault and staircase were found beneath it. It took four field seasons to clear away the rubble that clogged the passage, but eventually a large crypt was found some eighty feet below the top of the temple. Within the funerary chamber was a monolithic sarcophagus richly decorated with carvings. When the stone lid was raised, the coffin revealed the skeleton of a tall man between forty and fifty years of age with a life-size jade mosaic mask on his face. The burial furnishings included a glittering multitude of jade figures and two finely modeled stucco heads.

Palenque, due to its spectacular forest setting, is considered by many the most entrancing of the Maya ceremonial cities. In this aerial view, the palace compound is in the foreground, the Temple of the Inscriptions at right. It was in the latter in 1952 that Dr. Alberto Ruz discovered the great funerary crypt, a restoration of which is shown at far left. Below is a bas relief from Yaxchilán, a remote site near Palenque known for the exceptional quality of its stone carvings. Dated September 17, 726, it shows a priest (left) receiving a jaguar's head from a richly adorned personage.

Scenes from a reconstruction of the
Bonampak murals include a nobleman
(below), dignitaries watching a procession
of musicians (center), and the torture
scene that caused Mayanists to reexamine
their assumption that the Maya were a
purely pacific people (far right).

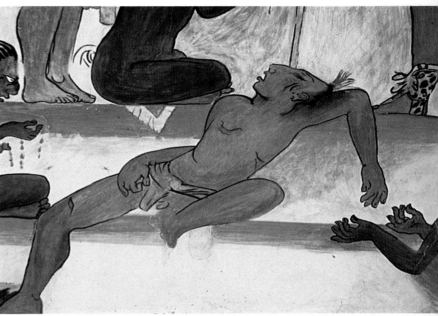

Before Dr. Ruz's discovery, it had been uniformly maintained that Mesoamerican pyramids were unlike those in Egypt in one essential respect — they did not contain tombs. But after the Palenque find, other tombs were located in Tikal, also within pyramids. Still other beliefs about the Maya were unsettled in 1946 when a party of explorers, led by the North American photographer Giles Healey, came upon the small temple of Bonampak, also in Chiapas and not far from Palenque. Before the discovery of Bonampak, Mayanists had contended that the Classic Maya knew little of war and bloodshed and did not practice bloody sacrifices. But at Bonampak vivid murals, which can be dated to about A.D. 800, showed warlike scenes in which prisoners were brutally tortured, some having their nails torn from their fingers.

Bonampak notwithstanding, most of the evidence does suggest that the Classic Maya were predominantly pacific, that orderly intercourse between autonomous ceremonial centers was the rule, not the exception. What is less clear is the precise nature of those centers. Were they cities like Teotihuacán? Jorge E. Hardoy, an Argentine scholar, has recently made a detailed study of all pre-Columbian cities, examining with particular care the great site of Tikal in the Petén of Guatemala. The site has been meticulously excavated by the University of Pennsylvania, and has been mapped with a thoroughness comparable to Millon's at Teotihuacán. In the course of the dig, Pennsylvania archaeologists unearthed a million-odd potsherds and more than 100,000 tools and other objects found in a six-square-mile area dotted with 3,000 separate constructions — confirming that Tikal was the largest of all

Maya centers. But was it a city? William R. Coe, the director of the Pennsylvania campaign, concluded that at least ten thousand people were permanent residents of Tikal and that the centers did have many elements of an urban level or way of living, though he added: "But whether it was a city or not will undoubtedly be argued for a long time to come."

For his part, Hardoy adjudged that Tikal's monumental architecture displays a character "totally different from that created by the Olmecs, by the builders of Teotihuacán and, centuries later, by the Aztecs." The Tikal temples loom in isolation, with little axial connection, and the density of the resident population in no way compares with that of Teotihuacán. "I am inclined to think," writes Hardoy, "that the Maya had no need to build cities. The labor entailed in building and then inhabiting them would undoubtedly have been disproportionate to the limited benefits they could provide." Though the verdict is subject to revision, there is at this point little reason to dispute Teotihuacán's claim to being the earliest true American city.

Whether they were real urban settlements, the Maya centers were unquestionably an extraordinary achievement. Yet, inexplicably, they were abandoned. J. Eric Thompson, the distinguished English Mayanist, provides the roll of the last datable hieroglyphic inscriptions: "Copán ceased to erect hieroglyphic monuments in A.D. 800, the year Charlemagne was crowned in Rome; Quiriguá, Piedras Negras, and Etzna (in Campeche) followed suit in A.D. 810; Tila gave up in A.D. 830; Oxtinkok's last date is A.D. 849; Tikal and Seibal dedicated their last stelae in A.D. 869, two years before Alfred came to the throne; Uaxactun, Xultun, Xaman-

tún, and Chichén Itzá kept going until A.D. 869 (the last perhaps a little later). La Muñeca, not far from the border between Campeche and Petén, has a stela which probably commemorates A.D. 909, and possibly the same date may be recorded on the latest stela at Naranjo. Just possibly a crude stela at San Lorenzo, near La Muñeca, carries a Maya date equivalent to A.D. 928, the latest of all. Five years later, the Magyar hordes were turned back at the battle of Unstrut, and European civilization was saved."

Why? The candid answer is that nobody knows why the Maya abruptly abandoned what had cost them so much effort to achieve. "Almost the only fact surely known about the downfall of Classic Maya civilization is that it really happened," writes Michael Coe. "All the rest is pure conjecture." Theories abound: epidemic diseases like yellow fever; agricultural calamities; invasion and internal revolution; even earthquake or a possibly unbalanced sex ratio. Suffice it to say that none of the theories accords with provable facts (yellow fever, for example, was unknown until the arrival of the Europeans). It happened. The Classic noon was over. A time of transition was under way.

The woman at right with a codex indicates Maya literacy in A.D. 550–900, when few Europeans, male or female, could read. Below is a part of the Madrid Codex, a rare surviving Maya document.

Overleaf:

These pottery figures from Jaina (an island off the west coast of Yucatán that served as a necropolis) and other nearby sites may have been portraits of the deceased. At left is a woman of rank with an elaborate coiffure; opposite her are figures representing various imposing individuals, including a ballplayer (top center).

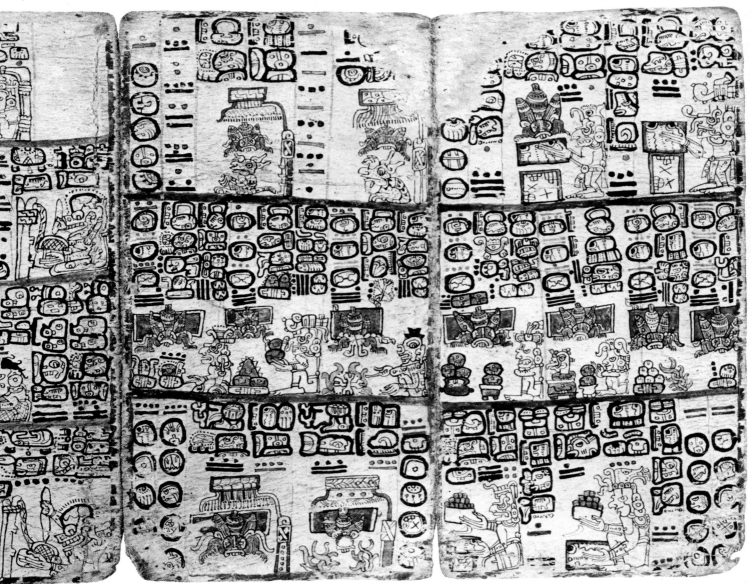

V
Blood and Flowers

Invasion, conquest, and the dim beginnings of recorded history — these are the motifs of the Mesoamerican period known as the Postclassic, dating from around A.D. 900 to the arrival of Cortés in 1519. During these years, two great militarist empires — those of the Toltecs and the Aztecs — mastered the central highlands, while other warrior peoples were dominant elsewhere. The tranquillity of the Classic era was succeeded by an epoch of incessant strife and by the advent of human sacrifice on a gruesome scale. Yet traces of the ancient civility persisted; the Postclassic era was very much like our own, a mingling of barbarity and enlightenment.

The collapse of the three major Classic civilizations was roughly comparable to the fall of the Western Roman Empire. Dying cities were overrun by virile newcomers, who, like the Goths and Vandals, absorbed some of the civilized ways of the peoples they had vanquished. As in Europe, religion served as a linking bridge — the older gods were adopted by the invaders. And again as in the Europe of the Dark Ages, myths and historical facts were entwined in tribal chronicles of battles and heroes. For the first time in Mesoamerica, we possess the actual names of real personages, and even a few ascertainable dates flicker in the fog. Many of the stories concern a people called the Toltecs.

Who were the Toltecs? By diligent inquiry, the early Spanish friars learned that the Aztecs were latecomers to the Valley of Mexico, that they had been preceded by another famous tribe speaking the same Nahuatl language. The Toltecs reputedly were magnificent builders, skilled agriculturalists, and even workers of metal — so considerable was their reputation that in time the word "Toltec" became a synonym for "master builder," "artist," and "civilized person." But the friars were not the sole recorders of Toltec history; an important early account was written by an Indian prince named Fernando de Alva Ixtlilxochitl (pronounced eeshlee-sʜow-cheel), of the royal line of the kingdom of Texcoco, an area near Teotihuacán.

After the Conquest, Ixtlilxochitl became an interpreter for the Spanish viceroy. By virtue of his birth and position, he had access to a large collection of Indian manuscripts as well as to the sages of his own tribe, and from these sources he wrote a history, in Spanish, of the Mesoamerican past. He penetrated, as Prescott writes, "into the mysterious depths of antiquity, where light and darkness melt into each other, and where everything is still further liable to distortion, as seen through the misty medium of hieroglyphics."

According to Ixtlilxochitl, in remote times, after the fall of Teotihuacán, various warlike peoples from the north burst into the central plateau of Mexico. Among these was the tribe known as the Toltecs. The Toltec chief was called Mixcóatl, meaning "Cloud Serpent," and he led his people into the Valley of Mexico around A.D. 900, one of the earliest quasi-historical dates in Mesoamerican history. Mixcóatl and his tribe settled in a place called Colhuacán, and there, around 935 or 947, a son was born to Cloud Serpent. The child's name was Ce Acatl Topíltzin, or "Our Lord One Reed," and he was to become the most famous figure in pre-Hispanic history, a Mesoamerican King Arthur. Topíltzin had to flee into exile when his father was murdered, but he later avenged the great king and returned to rule in his own right. He was not only a secular ruler but also a high priest of the god Quetzalcoatl, whose name he adopted, thereby creating a source of endless confusion. Under his leadership, the Toltecs founded a new capital, which they named Tollán (today called Tula), meaning "Place of the Reeds."

Topíltzin, or Quetzalcoatl, who was described as being fair-faced and bearded, turned Tula into a demiparadise. In the words of Fray Bernardino de Sahagún, whose account complements that of Ixtlilxochitl, Tula was favored with a golden age:

> Under his [Topíltzin's] rule, maize was plentifully available, gourds were very plump, an armful in circumference, and the maize cobs were of a gigantic size . . . . Cotton of all colors was harvested, red, yellow, brown, white, green, blue and orange . . . cocoa trees of the most diverse colors grew plentifully. . . . Quetzalcoatl's subjects were exceedingly rich and they lacked for nothing. There was no hunger, maize was not lacking, indeed, it was so abundant that the small maize cobs were not consumed but used for heating baths.

Yet in this Camelot the king had enemies; he was later cruelly tricked into becoming drunk and corrupt and was finally forced to flee to the south, toward the land of the Maya.

A fanciful story, no doubt, and modern scholars were properly dubious. But the myth proved to contain a solid kernel of fact, and the memory of Quetzalcoatl was to play a part in the Spanish Conquest of Mexico. One of the careful readers of the story of the Toltecs was a Frenchman, Claude Joseph Désiré Charnay, who decided to try and find the site of Tula. Charnay is typical of the quirky, self-taught explorers who have contributed much to our knowledge of ancient

Mexico — he was born in 1828, near Lyons, and was a young teacher of French in New Orleans when he made his first visit to Mexico in 1857. He climbed the snow-tipped peak of Popocatepetl, and there encountered the first enthralling artifacts of pre-Columbian peoples. In the 1880's, he returned to Mexico as an archaeological explorer with the financial help of the Franco-American tycoon Paul P. Lorillard (after whom the grateful Charnay named a Maya city).

Charnay began his quest for Tula, logically enough, at a present-day village with the same name in the state of Hidalgo, about fifty miles north of Mexico City. Tula is today easily accessible via a modern superhighway. In Charnay's time, the trip was an arduous one; he recounts passing through endless, flat fields and past fortresslike churches over the worst road he had ever encountered. ("It is a wonder how we advance at all, for the wheels of our carriage almost disappear into the ruts," he complained.) At Tula, he came upon a small town of some one thousand persons near the obvious remains of ancient temples. He excavated and unearthed fragments of three Atlantean figures — statues of warriors used as supports — as well as the ruins of palaces, plazas, and ball courts. In a book published in 1884, Charnay announced his extraordinary finds — but no one was listening.

An admittedly flamboyant character, Charnay was ignored as an unreliable romantic. Until the 1940's, most scholars insisted that the site of fabled Tula was probably at Cholula or Teotihuacán — even the brilliant George Vaillant stubbornly stuck to the latter identification. Finally, in 1940, Mexican archaeologists directed by Jorge Acosta began a major dig at Tula and confirmed that the self-taught Charnay was right. The ancient city was not only a splendid one but clearly the seat of a warrior kingdom, the best indication being the multitude of depictions of armed soldiers and the comparative infrequency of depictions of the gods.

At Tula, too, excavators found much pottery attesting to the artistic influence of another warlike tribe, the Mixtecs, who were said to be the master metalworkers of Postclassic Mesoamerica. The Mixtecs called themselves Nusabi, or "People of the Rain," and claimed that their tribe originated in the high, foggy Sierras of Oaxaca. The evidence of archaeology shows that the Mixtec culture dates back to at least 648 B.C. and that this fierce but aesthetically gifted people came to dominate the Valley of Oaxaca around A.D. 1300, displacing the Zapotecs, who had created Monte Albán.

The Mixtecs made the ancient shrine their own, even to the extent of reusing the Zapotec tombs. In 1932, Dr. Alfonso Caso, the dean of Mexican archaeology, was engaged in clearing the vast site of Monte Albán. He was sifting through Mixtec burials when, in Tomb No. 7, he came upon the intact grave of a noble of high rank and his slaughtered servants. No richer find has been made in the New World; it established that although the Mixtecs were indifferent builders, they were superlative goldsmiths and jewelers. For the first time, sculptured gold was found that substantiated the description of the incredible treasures found by the Spanish conquistadors. There were masks and ornaments of beaten gold and quantities of carved jade, turquoise mosaics, a rock crystal goblet, objects of amber, jet, and coral — and a pearl the size of a pigeon's

egg. The cache of hundreds of fine pieces (now handsomely displayed in the fine local museum in Oaxaca) also contained a collection of jaguar bones on which mythological and historical scenes were carved.

These scenes intrigued Caso, and he undertook a study of Mixtec codices — folded deerskin books written before the Conquest that contained the history of royal houses in a combination of pictographic and rebus writing. In a tour de force of modern scholarship, Caso was able to carry back Mixtec history as far as A.D. 692, the earliest point in the annals of any Mesoamerican people. Since the Mixtecs used a numerical and calendrical system common to much of ancient Mexico, Caso was also able to establish the actual dates of the events described.

We thus have a historical narrative of the lives and times of the great Mixtec monarchs, most notably that of a king called Eight Deer, so named, as were most Indians, by the day of his birth (see box, page 83). In the biography of Eight Deer, we discover that royal politics in Mesoamerica was much like that in most other places where absolute monarchs ruled — a matter of extinguishing rival brothers, marrying wisely for dynastic reasons, and avoiding all wars that could not be won.

Eight Deer was born in 1011 and died in 1063. During his lifetime he married five times, fathered many children, and won countless battles, extending his Mixtec realm south to the Pacific coast and north possibly as far as Cholula. His father was a king, and while still a youth Eight Deer took part in many wars. In 1045, he was invested as king himself by having a royal button inserted in his nose, probably by a Toltec king or

priest at Tula — collateral evidence of the power of the Toltec capital. In his many battles, Eight Deer took care to sacrifice the males of the royal families he subdued, while he or his sons married their widows and daughters.

A major campaign involved a town called Xipe-Bundle, so called after its hieroglyph in the codices, which show a bundle of religious articles associated with Xipe (pronounced shee-pay), a fertility god. A crisis arose when the ruler of Xipe-Bundle, a Mixtec king named Eleven Wind, died in 1047. One of Eleven Wind's wives was the full sister of a half brother of Eight Deer and was thus a claimant to the throne. But Eleven Wind also had three children by Eight Deer's half sister, two of whom were boys who might also succeed Eleven Wind. To prevent these dangerous kinfolk from ascending a throne from which they might threaten his own dynasty, Eight Deer allied himself with a Toltec warlord, Four Tiger, and war ensued. In a preliminary campaign, Eight Deer captured his half brother, who was promptly dispatched. Before long, Eight Deer had all the other heirs in his control. The two half nephews were killed, respectively, in a ritual sacrifice and a gladiatorial combat. Eight Deer then married the surviving half niece, Thirteen Serpent, who later bore him three daughters and two sons, one of whom was destined to become a Mixtec king. Finally, there was another son of Eleven Wind's, named Four Wind, whose mother had no blood tie to Eight Deer; this boy was spared.

If this seems a dark world, one need only recall the contemporary world of Macbeth and the fierce clans of Scotland, in which professing Christians engaged in

Xochipilli, the Prince of Flowers, was the Aztec god of games and love and summer and was always portrayed with butterflies and flowers. In the generally grim pantheon of Aztec gods, he is one of the few associated with festivity and gaiety. His cult, however, was not exclusively flowers, for even he is more usually portrayed holding a staff on which is impaled a human heart.

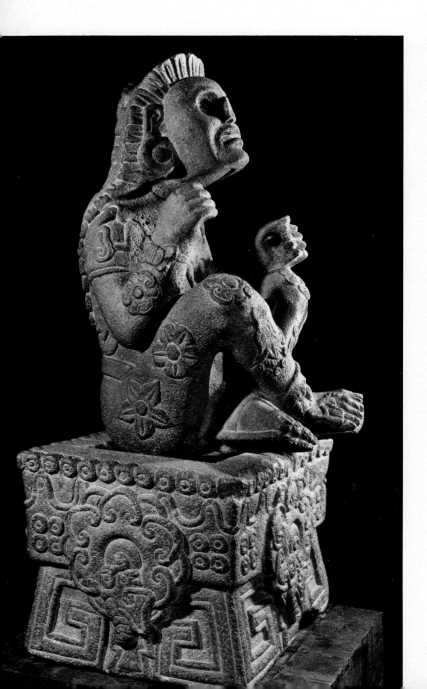

dynastic wars hardly less violent. The Postclassic Mesoamerican kings sat on thrones of blood and accepted fully that death was the price of defeat. In 1063, Eight Deer attacked the native capital of the last of his five wives and lost the battle. He was taken captive and ritually sacrificed, and no doubt he died without any complaints.

In terms of sheer magnitude of ferocity, however, the Mixtecs paled by comparison with the Aztecs, whose civilization was a unique tapestry of blood and flowers, of the demonic and the sublime. There is no New World culture whose folkways are at once so fascinating and so repellent as those of the Aztecs, who loom like the Golden Horde of Genghis Khan in the history of Mesoamerica.

The Aztecs were conscious of being latecomers into civilized Mexico; in his first conversation with Cortés the emperor Moctezuma told the Spaniard: "From the records which we have long possessed and which are handed down from our ancestors, it is known that no one, neither I nor the others who inhabit this land of Anahuac [the Valley of Mexico] are native to it. We are strangers and we come from far outer parts." Tribal records related that the Aztecs belonged to a northern barbarian people collectively known as Chichimecs, which was proudly translated as meaning "Sons of the Dogs." As an early Spanish chronicler was told: "Know that when our ancestors lived in the wilds, in the thorny deserts, they lived by the bow and arrow — if they were not assiduous, they did not eat — and that was in the days of those godlike Chichimecs, our ancestors."

These same children of the dogs gave their name to

modern Mexico, founded an empire of barbaric splendor, and created on the very lakes in the Valley of Mexico an island city so large and spectacular that it amazed its Spanish conquerors. The Aztecs first entered Mexico in the twelfth century — 1168 is the traditional date — at the time of the fall of the Toltec empire. A particularly aggressive branch of the Aztec nation, a tribe known as the Mexica, came to settle on a headland rising on swampy Lake Texcoco, a bluff named Chapultepec, or "Grasshopper Hill," so called because of its shape when seen from the side.

The Mexica Aztecs were then a lowly tribe, little better than vassals to stronger neighbors, though they worshiped a fearsome war god of their own, Huitzilopochtli (pronounced wheetzeel-o-POCH-lee), meaning "Left-handed Hummingbird." The early Aztec settlement at Chapultepec met its end in a terrible disaster when most of its people were massacred in a tribal war. This terminated the first firm habitation at the future site of Mexico City, but the Aztecs were reassured that the gods would give them a sign as to where they should reestablish their capital.

Specifically, it was prophesied that the site would be identified by a cactus tree on which an eagle would be seen devouring its prey. And lo! an Aztec scout came upon a thicket in which he saw an eagle gripping a serpent in its beak at the base of a cactus tree in one of the boggy pools near Lake Texcoco. The pool's waters were chalk white — the color of sacrifice. Thus was founded Tenochtitlán, the future Mexico City, and so durable is the founding myth that an eagle mounted on a cactus, gripping a snake in its beak, remains an emblem of the Republic of Mexico today.

THE AZTEC CALENDAR

The Aztecs actually had two calendars, an agriculturally oriented one of 360 days (with five additional days of ill omen added at the end) and a more ancient ritual calendar, the *tonalpohualli*, found throughout Mesoamerica. This calendar was important for ceremonial purposes and for reading signs and portents, and virtually every Indian included as part of his name his date of birth according to its calculations. The calendar consisted of a series of twenty signs and thirteen numbers that followed in rigid sequence for a cycle of 260 days. The signs were

Alligator	Monkey
Wind	Grass
House	Reed
Lizard	Jaguar
Serpent	Eagle
Death	Vulture
Deer	Earthquake
Rabbit	Flint
Water	Rain
Dog	Flower

The cycle began with One Alligator followed by Two Wind, Three House, Four Lizard up to Thirteen Reed, after which the number would revert again to one, beginning One Jaguar, Two Eagle, and so forth. It would continue through all its permutations ending on the 260th day with Thirteen Flower, and a new cycle would start again with One Alligator.

The perilous trek of the Aztecs as they made their way from the land of the Chichimecs, their ancestors, to found Tenochtitlán is quaintly portrayed here with footsteps showing the route they followed. The phantasmagoric beasts they face include birds as big as jaguars and rabbits larger still. Although most of the tribe members seem assured of reaching their destination, the two Indians at upper left have apparently succumbed to a jaguar.

cuauhtla

rexcalco

Within a few generations, this tribe of wretched squatters, derisively described as "the people whose face nobody knows," became the imperial masters of central Mexico and extended their influence as far south as Guatemala. The Aztecs were ruthless and disciplined warriors and were led by a succession of brilliant chiefs. But this of itself does not explain their explosive expansion — there was a further vital factor.

The Aztecs saw themselves as a chosen people, a race consecrated to the sun, with a special obligation to their tribal god, Huitzilopochtli, who could only be kept alive by human sacrifice. To feed the god, war was essential in order to obtain a continuing supply of sacrificial captives. This impelled the Aztecs to conduct what they called *xochiyáotl,* or "flowery wars," in which the purpose was not conquest but the capture of prisoners for the altars of their insatiable god. When the Great Temple of Tenochtitlán was dedicated, no fewer than 20,000 victims obtained in a flowery war were offered to Huitzilopochtli.

The Aztecs were ever alert to portents. It is difficult for a secular contemporary to imagine himself in the god-haunted cosmos of pre-Hispanic peoples, to conceive of a time when the simplest of events — the shape of a cloud, the cycle of the seasons, the chance color of a mountain dawn — were filled with secret significance, containing messages that the wise could decode. Even the calendar was a book of revelations, with each day possessing its peculiar attributes. In his invaluable history, the friar Diego Durán relates any number of episodes in which the Aztecs or their rivals were moved to act by the language of portents.

At one point, Durán writes, the Aztecs were warring with a people called the Chalca, and both armies were readying for battle when, in the middle of the night, the owls began a spectral dialogue. One owl hooted: *"Tiacan, tiacan!"* ("Mighty, mighty!"), and another answered: *"Nocne, nocne!"* ("Alas, alas!"). Both the Aztecs and the Chalca were terrified by the cries, taking them to be an ill omen, and while they trembled, the two owls continued to talk. *"Tetec, tetec!"* ("Cut, cut!") one owl said, and the other replied: *"Yollo, yollo!"* ("Hearts, hearts!"). To which the first owl added: *"Quetechpol chichil, quetechpol chichil!"* ("Red throats, red throats!"). And the second owl said, *"Chalca! Chalca!"* (O men of Chalco! O men of Chalco!").

Upon hearing this, an Aztec chief declared: "O Aztecs, listen to the owls, hear how they announce our victory! Some divine thing moves these birds to hoot in such a manner. . . . It is fated, O Aztecs! Courage and strength! Let us not in our weakness lose what has been sent to us from above." And the Aztecs duly prevailed over the Chalca.

To the ancient Mexicans, the natural world was an unstable and menacing place, and it was rendered only a bit more sensible by a highly complicated system of religion. Not only were there hundreds of gods, but specific deities could wear many guises, varying from place to place and time to time. So confusing was the system that even before the Spanish arrived, efforts were made to simplify and reform the theological tangle. A king of Texcoco named Nezahaulcóyotl introduced the worship of an invisible god who was in the highest realm of heaven and on whom all things depended. The king built a special temple to the invisible god, and in this sanctuary there was no image of the god since he was a pure idea. Of this remarkable reform, Alfonso Caso writes: "Naturally this single god of Nezahaulcóyotl did not have much following, nor did he affect the religious life of the people. The gods of the philosophers have never been popular, for they arise from the need of a logical explanation of the universe, while the common people require less abstract gods who will satisfy their need for love and protection."

Despite the menace of their cosmos, there is a certain poetic loveliness in various Mesoamerican accounts of the creation, and there is evidence, too, that the ancient religion had an ethical component elevating it above mere animism or superstition. A prevalent tradition held that all the gods sprang from two creator deities — one masculine, one feminine — known as Ometecuhtli, or "Two Lord," and Omecíhuatl, or "Two Lady," who dwelled in Omeyocan, "The Place of the Two." One version asserts that these creators had four sons to whom they entrusted the creation of other gods, the world, and man. The four sons were Quetzalcoatl, Tezcatlipoca, Xipe, and Huitzilopochtli.

Of these four, Quetzalcoatl, or "Plumed Serpent," was deemed a beneficent deity, a founder of agriculture and the arts, while Tezcatlipoca, or "Smoking Mirror," was the patron of darkness, evil, and sorcery. The history of the world, so it was believed, was the tale of the struggle between these contrary deities. A colorful creation myth asserts that in the very earliest times Tezcatlipoca reigned as the sun over the newly created world and over the first men, who were a race of giants. But Quetzalcoatl struck him with a staff, and

The passage of the seasons and the disappearance
and rebirth of solar and stellar bodies were of
consuming interest to the early peoples of
Mesoamerica. Here, from a pre-Hispanic codex, is
one of a remarkable pictorial series depicting the
voyage of Venus into the underworld — when it was
invisible from the earth — until its return as the
embodiment of the heart of Quetzalcoatl.

the sun god fell into the water, turning into a jaguar who promptly devoured the first men. This happened on a day known as Four Jaguar.

Now it was Quetzalcoatl's turn to be the sun, and the jaguar avenged himself by striking his rival down with his paw, causing a great wind to arise that decimated a second race of men. This occurred on the day Four Wind. The creator gods now decided that Tlaloc, god of rain and celestial fire, should be the sun. But the envious Quetzalcoatl caused fire to rain down on earth, killing the third race of men. The day this took place was Four Rain. Then Quetzalcoatl chose Tlaloc's sister as a new sun goddess — she was known as Chalchiuhtlicue, or "Lady of the Jade Skirts," and was the deity of water. The vexed Tezcatlipoca made it rain so hard that the earth was flooded and a fourth race of men drowned or turned into fish — this happened on the day Four Water. Finally Quetzalcoatl and Tezcatlipoca joined hands and raised the earth so that it might be dry and that a race of men might once again dwell there.

There are many variations of this creation myth, but what most have in common is a conception of multiple creations, a ceaseless process of renewal and regeneration. This conception took literal, if grim, form in the worship of Xipe Tótec, "Our Lord the Flayed One," the god of spring. Xipe is easily recognizable because he is shown wearing a second human skin and seems to possess two mouths. He was worshiped by flaying a victim, whose skin would then be worn by a priest, thus symbolizing both the advent of spring and the new coat of vegetation.

Joined to this deeply felt sense of renewal was a conviction that human behavior was governed by divinely ordained codes of right conduct, and that a respect for the gods would find its reward in the afterlife. However horrible Aztec human sacrifices may seem to us, death on the altar did not seem so dreadful to the victim. There was a dignity, even a redeeming tenderness, in the relations between the victor and victim in battle; the latter was not degraded, and the former seldom showed a lust for blood. When an Aztec took a prisoner, he would say, "Here is my well-beloved son." The captive would reply, "Here is my revered father." The annals of the early friars recount a number of instances in which brave enemies were offered their freedom by their Aztec captors; they voluntarily chose the sacrificial knife instead.

To be sure, some rituals were irredeemably barbaric, for example, the sacrifice of children to Tlaloc, or the grisly fire ceremony in which captives were broiled in embers, their hearts torn from their blistered bodies while they were still agonizingly alive. But there was also the poignant ceremony honoring Tezcatlipoca. For this sacrifice, the best-looking and bravest prisoner was chosen a year in advance, and during that time he became the incarnation of the god himself. He was attended by devoted priests, who accompanied him as he strolled about playing lovely melodies on a flute. Shortly before his execution four girls were chosen to be his companions; they would weep copiously on his last day, when he would lead a joyous procession to the temple. In mounting it, he would pause and break a flute at each step, a melancholy token of the end of his reign. After his heart was ripped from his breast, his body was carried down the stairs, not flung to the

In this detail from a post-Conquest codex, priests and laymen sacrifice two victims to Huitzilopochtli, god of war, to ensure continued success in the wars that were fought to provide the victims for just such sacrifices. Above, right, is a stone effigy in the shape of a gargantuan jaguar. In it were placed the hearts of the sacrificial victims.

bottom in the usual manner. His skull, however, was strung on a rack with all the rest.

Jacques Soustelle, the French anthropologist who saw something of modern cruelty during his years as an official in colonial Algeria, says in mitigation of the Aztecs: "At the height of their career the Romans shed more blood in their circuses and for their amusement than ever the Aztecs did before their idols. The Spaniards, so sincerely moved by the cruelty of native priests, nevertheless massacred, burnt, mutilated and tortured with a perfectly clear conscience." Or as Prescott adds, death on the Aztec altars opened a clear path to paradise to the victim, whereas the Holy Inquisition "branded its victims with infamy in this world and consigned them to everlasting perdition in the next."

Indeed, there was a special heaven for the Aztecs who died in battle or on the *téchcatl*, the sacrificial stone. This paradise was called Tonatiuhichan, or "House of the Sun," and there brave warriors would fight sham battles in gardens filled with flowers — and after four years, these honored souls would return to earth as hummingbirds to feed upon the nectar of flowers. Those who died by drowning, lightning, or diseases considered related to the water gods went to Tlalocan, the paradise of Tlaloc, where food of all kinds abounds. A vivid mural at Teotihuacán, where Tlaloc was depicted more than any other deity, shows the delights of Tlalocan, where the lucky dead loll blissfully on the banks of a lush river or join in exuberant games in the water itself.

Altogether, there were in the Mesoamerican cosmogony a total of nine hells and thirteen heavens; the

At left is an Aztec rendition of a ball court and opposite is Chichén Itzá, a late Maya city with the most famous ball court of all, a portion of which can be seen at far right. Little is known of the rules of the game, except that a rubber ball was to be propelled by back, hip, or shoulder through a ring high on the side of the court. One authority has it that a player who accomplished this could then rip the garments off any spectator he could catch.

souls of the dead underwent a series of magical trials to determine their reward or punishment. Just as ancient Greeks would place a coin in the mouths of the dead — so that they could pay a fare to Charon and be ferried across the Styx — so charms and amulets were buried with the Indian dead to help in the trials of the after-life. (In fact, the very first trial was to cross a river, and sometimes a dog was placed in a burial to help his master swim the swift waters.)

There was, in other words, a system of divine sanctions to enforce right conduct. Moreover, there were voices raised against the bloody practice of mass human sacrifices, the most notable being that of Topíltzin, or Quetzalcoatl, the priest-king of Tula. It is recorded that Topíltzin abhorred human sacrifices and taught his people to kill butterflies instead. His peaceful cult seems to echo the earlier ways of the Classic era, suggesting that the conflict between the life-giving Quetzalcoatl and the satanic Tezcatlipoca embodies a conflict between two ethical outlooks. While one should not overstate this duality, the conflict does find mythic expression in the story of what eventually happened to the fair-faced Topíltzin.

Legends assert that Tezcatlipoca was mightily angered by the Toltec philosopher-king and sought to corrupt him by various wicked stratagems. Once Tezcatlipoca appeared before Topíltzin in the disguise of an old man and tricked him into drinking a malignant potion that made the king drunk. The dark god's magic caused many other misfortunes, including epidemics, forest fires, and a rain of thunderbolts in the form of stone axes. Whereupon the despondent king decided to burn his palaces, bury his treasures, and leave Tula.

According to Fray Bernardino de Sahagún, the king sailed from the coast of Veracruz aboard a raft of intertwined snakes, setting his course for an ancestral homeland located in the east. Some say that upon returning he had himself burned alive, and his heart became the morning star. Others assert that he did not die, but vowed instead to return to Tula.

There were two momentous sequels to the myth. The first was the discovery that the Toltecs had indeed made their way east at about the time of the collapse of Tula and had established a new kingdom among the Maya in Yucatán. Charnay, the first excavator of Tula, was also among the first to remark on an uncanny coincidence — that much of the Postclassic architecture in Chichén Itzá clearly resembles that of the buildings in Tula, even though the two sites are some eight hundred miles apart. According to Maya chronicles, in around the tenth century A.D. the Yucatán was invaded by a people called the Itzá, who were said to come from a place named Tulapán and whose chief was the high priest Kukulkán, the Maya word for Feathered Serpent. Modern investigations have fully confirmed that the Toltecs settled in Chichén Itzá, adorning that Maya city with extensive colonnades, Atlantean warriors with Toltec costumes, grim skull racks, and scores of depictions of Quetzalcoatl.

A second sequel was still more fateful. It had been foretold that Topíltzin would return from the east in the year One Reed, which falls every fifty-two years in the Mesoamerican calendar. In 1519, a Spanish adventurer named Hernán Cortés, drawn by rumors of a fabled Indian kingdom, set sail for the coast of Veracruz. He landed in the year One Reed.

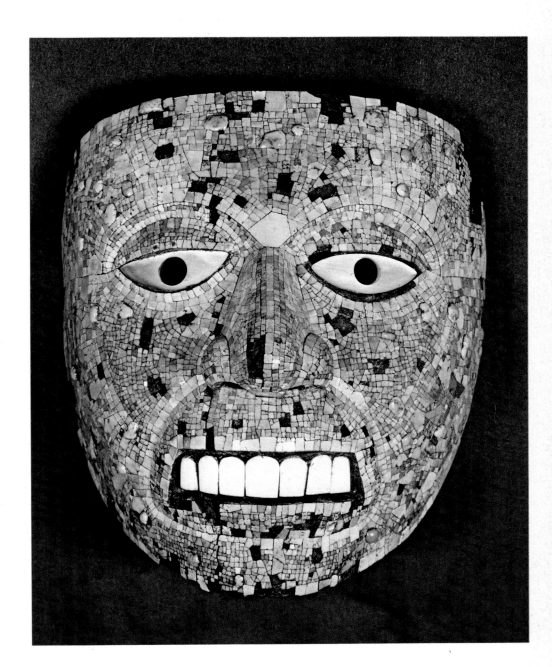

The bizarre artistry of the Aztecs is graphically displayed in these three mosaic masks. The lignite and turquoise mask inlaid over a human skull at far left is considered one of the most extraordinary of its kind and is one of the major prizes in the British Museum's Mesoamerican collection; it is thought to represent the god Tezcatlipoca. Tlaloc appears in an elaborate headdress at left. The mask above is thought to represent the powerful Quetzalcoatl.

VI
The Broken Spears

Gazing on such wonderful sights, we did not know what to say, or whether what appeared before us was real, for on one side, on the land, there were great cities, and in the lake ever so many more, and the lake itself was crowded with canoes, and in the Causeway were many bridges at intervals, and in front of us stood the great City of Mexico, and we — we did not even number four hundred soldiers!"

So recalled one of the conquistadors, Bernal Díaz del Castillo, who took part in the entire Mexican campaign and who, when he was eighty-four and without sight or hearing, dictated a memorable account of what he had witnessed. Like all the Spaniards, Bernal Díaz was utterly unprepared for his first glimpse of Tenochtitlán, the magnificent Aztec capital. To be sure, the tiny army had already come upon Indian cities of unexpected size and grandeur during its march inland from Veracruz. The Spaniards were also well aware that the emperor Moctezuma was the richest, most powerful lord in all Mexico. The king had sent them sumptuous gifts, including (Bernal Díaz relates) "a wheel like the sun, big as a cartwheel, with many sorts of pictures on it, the whole of fine gold, and a wonderful thing to behold." Yet these were only hints of what was to come; the conquistadors had small reason to guess that Tenochtitlán and its satellite city Tlaltelolco would consist of 60,000 houses and have as many as 300,000 inhabitants — five times the size of Henry VIII's London. What made the Aztec capital more marvelous still was that it rested on built-up flats in shallow lakes and was webbed with canals in which floating gardens bloomed. (The modern visitor can still get an idea of how the ancient city looked by visit-

scribes each of them, and thus we know that a gray mare called "La Rabona" was "very handy, and a good charger," whereas a light chestnut horse with white stockings was "not much good." The intimidating potential of the horse was apparent shortly after the fleet made its first landfalls on the island of Cozumel and along the coast of Tabasco. After a skirmish with the Tabascan Indians, the Spaniards arranged for peace talks with the caciques, or chiefs. Before the meeting took place, Cortés confided to some of his men: "Do you know, gentlemen, that it seems to me that the Indians are terrified of the horses and may think that they and our cannon alone make war on them. I have thought of something that will confirm this belief, and that is to bring the mare belonging to Juan Sedeño and to tie her up where I am standing and also to bring the stallion of Ortíz the musician, which is very excitable, near enough to scent the mare, and when he has scented her to lead each of them off separately so that the Caciques who are coming shall not hear the horses' neighing as they approach, not until they are standing before me and are talking to me."

The plan was duly carried out, and when the Tabascan chiefs stood conferring with Cortés a cannon was fired, sending a ball buzzing into the hills; then the excitable stallion was brought out, and the horse began neighing wildly as it scented the mare standing behind Cortés and the chiefs. Cortés went to the stallion, pretended to talk with it, had it taken away, and then soothingly explained to the dumbfounded chiefs that he had told the horse not to be angry, that the Indians were friendly and wished to make peace.

Cortés was able to communicate with the Tabascans

thanks to an accident. In their first landfall, at Cozumel, the Spaniards encountered a shipwrecked countryman, Jerónimo de Aguilar, who had been living among the Indians for eight years and had learned their language. While among the Tabascans, Cortés acquired a second interpreter, an Indian princess who came to be known as Doña Marina, or Malinche, a young woman of considerable intelligence. She spoke Nahuatl as well as the languages of the Yucatán, which Aguilar understood and could translate into Spanish, thus enabling Cortés to negotiate, if by cumbersome means, when he and his forces began their advance into Mexico.

On Holy Thursday, 1519, the fleet arrived on the coast of Veracruz, and on Good Friday, the army disembarked. After Mass was celebrated, Cortés had his first encounter with the emissaries of Moctezuma, about whom he had already heard much in Tabasco. With the help of his two interpreters, the Spanish captain explained that he was a Christian and the vassal of the greatest king on earth and that he had come to this country because he had heard rumors of the great prince who ruled it. His wish, Cortés insisted, was to meet in friendship with Moctezuma and to trade with the Aztecs. As messengers carried his words back to the Aztec capital, Cortés began exploring. Near the coast he discovered the city of Cempoala, whose king, a fat cacique whom the Spaniard greeted with a great show of caressing and flattery, described the doleful state of Mexico under Aztec tyranny.

In the words of Bernal Díaz, the fat cacique, with a sigh, complained bitterly of the great Moctezuma, "saying that he had recently been brought under his yoke;

that all his gold and jewels had been carried off, and he and his people so grievously oppressed that they dared do nothing without Moctezuma's orders, for he was the Lord over many cities and countries, and ruled countless vassals and armies of warriors." Cortés promised the stout chief that he would punish the evildoers, the first hint of the master strategy of the Conquest, for Cortés saw that he could ally himself with the Indians who detested the Aztecs. It was in the guise of a liberator that Cortés was able to impose the alien despotism of Spain on the vast territory he was to name New Spain.

At this point, too, Cortés ordered his single boldest stroke — the destruction of his own ships. The commander became aware of a conspiracy within his army, led by those loyal to Governor Velázquez as they saw a voyage of exploration evolve into an unauthorized attempt at conquest. In secrecy, Cortés ordered the sinking of all but one of his vessels, and, according to one account, then said that any of his men who wished to return to Cuba could sail on the last boat. He then declared: "As for me, I have chosen my part, I will remain here while there is one to bear me company. If there be any so craven as to shrink from sharing the dangers of our glorious enterprise, let them go home, in God's name. There is still one vessel left. Let them take that and return to Cuba. They can tell there how they deserted their commander and their comrades, and patiently wait till we return loaded with the spoils of the Aztecs." Even the dissidents joined in the answering shout: "To Mexico! To Mexico!"

So the march inland began, and on August 31, 1519, the Spaniards crossed the frontiers of Tlaxcala, an

An Aztec artist represented Cortés with an outsized sword and cross. This was the New World's first encounter with the horse, which was to strike terror into Indian warriors. Along the bottom are glyphs recording the event and at the top, above Cortés's sword, is the character for One Reed, the fateful year 1519 in the Aztec calendar.

Indian state with an elective government whose leaders hated the Aztecs with particular venom. There was a fierce battle in which the Spaniards prevailed, and the adroit Cortés swiftly made the Tlaxcalans his principal allies. All the while the increasingly worried envoys of Moctezuma hurried back and forth — it was at Tlaxcala that the Spaniards were presented with sumptuous gifts from Moctezuma. Cortés dispatched these to his king, Charles V, along with a deftly self-serving letter in which he reached over the head of Velázquez to the Spanish court itself.

These events were being reported to the emperor Moctezuma II, ninth king of the Aztecs, a hero in nine battles, who had reigned since 1502. Moctezuma was then about forty years old; as Bernal Díaz describes him, he was "of good height and well proportioned, slender and spare of flesh. . . . His face was somewhat long, but cheerful, and he had good eyes and showed in his appearance and manner both tenderness and, when necessary, gravity." He lived in a spacious palace with a personal guard of two hundred nobles, and for each meal more than thirty dishes were prepared for him. But in all this splendor, the king was moody, nervous, and irresolute. In the years immediately before the Conquest, the Aztecs had been distressed by a concatenation of omens that defied priestly explanation: comets were seen by day, temples were damaged by lightning, monstrous people appeared on the streets of the capital, some with two heads. When Moctezuma ordered that a large stone be brought to him for the sacrifice and skinning of men, the stone upbraided the emperor's servants, saying: "Poor wretches! Why do you labor in vain? Have I not told you that I will never

arrive in Mexico? Go tell Moctezuma that it is too late. He should have thought of this before. Now he no longer needs me; a terrible event, brought on by fate, is about to happen!" No less upsetting, a strange bird, resembling a crane, was brought before Moctezuma. It had a mirror on its head, and when the emperor peered into the glass, he saw men running across a plain mounted on animals that looked like deer. The ruler cried to his magicians: "Can you explain what I have seen? Creatures like human beings, running and fighting!" But when his priests looked into the mirror, they saw nothing.

And now, by an uncanny coincidence, Cortés arrived at Veracruz in 1519, or the year One Reed in the Aztec calendar, when it had been foretold that the bearded god-king Quetzalcoatl would return after four centuries in exile. The combination was simply too much for the great king, who vacillated as his oracles gave him conflicting advice. He was first urged to placate the strangers with gifts while forbidding their advance, which he did, and then was told that the Spaniards would surely meet their death at Cholula, the next kingdom on their line of march. Accordingly, Moctezuma sent his envoys to Cholula to plot an ambush of the invaders.

By the time Cortés arrived in Cholula, his small army had been generously reinforced by a fierce contingent of Tlaxcalans. At Cholula, the Spaniards were received with a show of friendship, and they marveled at the city's great pyramid and hundreds of whitewashed temples. But in talking with Cholulans, Malinche learned of the planned ambush and promptly alerted Cortés. The following day, the captain called a meeting with the Cholulan chiefs in a great plaza and

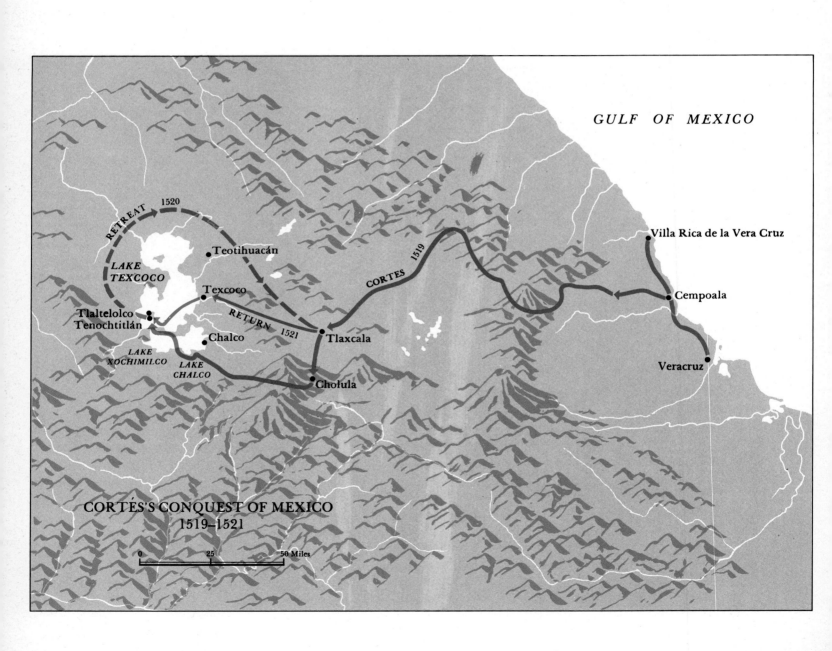

GULF OF MEXICO

Villa Rica de la Vera Cruz

Cempoala

Veracruz

RETREAT 1520

LAKE TEXCOCO

Teotihuacán

Texcoco

Tlaltelolco
Tenochtitlán

Chalco

RETURN 1521

Tlaxcala

CORTES 1519

LAKE XOCHIMILCO

LAKE CHALCO

Cholula

CORTÉS'S CONQUEST OF MEXICO
1519–1521

0   25   50 Miles

The levee, or ceremony of attiring an awakened potentate, was not confined to Bourbon France, as this fragment from an Aztec codex shows. Here a high dignitary is being adorned with his trappings of state while attendants look on. The rabbit at top, with a plant apparently sprouting from his head, may represent the maguey plant, from which alcoholic pulque is made.

accused them of perfidy. At a signal, the Spanish infantry posted around the square loosed its crossbows and fired its muskets, and the plaza was soon heaped with thousands of dead, the first massacre of the Conquest. But as Bernal Díaz drily relates: "This affair and punishment at Cholula became known throughout the provinces of New Spain, and if we had a reputation for valor before, from now on they took us for sorcerers, and said that no evil that was planned against us could be so hidden from us that it did not come to our knowledge, and on this account they showed us good will."

Thus a triumphal entry into Tenochtitlán was assured. There, in an idyllic interlude between bloodbaths, Cortés and his soldiers mingled peaceably with Moctezuma and his nobles. There have been few more extraordinary encounters in history, because the Spaniards found themselves in the capital of a brilliant native civilization, whose very existence was unknown, and were treated as godlike guests. There were great banquets, after which, Bernal Díaz reports, the Indians sucked on tubes filled with certain herbs called *tabaco.* The soldiers were shown the marvels of Moctezuma's palaces, his zoo, and his aviary. Every kind of bird was in the aviary, from the dazzling quetzals to fowl with stilted legs, their bodies and wings all of a crimson color. In one place, there were lions, tigers, jackals, and foxes, whose collective howl made an infernal noise, while in another (Bernal Díaz writes) there were poisonous snakes "which carry on their tails things that ring like bells." And the court was filled with jesters and buffoons, many of them dwarfs and humpbacks, who sang and danced and told witty aphorisms to Moc-

tezuma. Some of the temples were filled with books and narratives, all written on paper, and others had vast stores of weapons, including "stone knives which cut better than our swords."

But if all this was beguiling to the Spaniards, they were appalled when shown the great temple of Huitzilopochtli, its altars reeking of sacrificial blood. "The evil stench," asserts Bernal Díaz, "was less tolerable than that of the slaughterhouses in Castile." After descending the vast staircase of the main temple, the Spaniards came upon a smaller building nearby filled to the rafters with the skulls of victims. One of the soldiers calculated that there were 136,000 skulls.

Religion came up frequently in the earnest conversations between Cortés and Moctezuma. Though the Indian ruler showed a willingness to swear allegiance to the king of Spain, he was more stubborn on religious questions. Cortés patiently explained the mysteries of the Trinity and the Eucharist and condemned the practice of human sacrifice. For his part, Moctezuma listened politely, and then observed that it was less revolting to him to sacrifice human hearts than it was to eat the flesh and blood of God himself, as in the Mass. Regrettably, there is no record to inform us of how Cortés responded.

The idyllic interlude had to end. After a week in the Aztec citadel, the Spaniards became restive, and Cortés himself was uneasy about how long the amiable mood would last. There was always the danger of an incident involving a Spaniard or the high-spirited Tlaxcalans, who were now in daily contact with a people they loathed. Cortés conferred with his senior officers and reached a decision comparable in boldness

to his destruction of the ships — he concluded that the all-powerful Moctezuma should be seized and made a Spanish prisoner. A pretext for the act arose when Cortés learned that two Spanish soldiers garrisoned in Cholula had been murdered by the Aztecs. The commander asked for an audience with Moctezuma, and at this meeting the emperor was accused of complicity in the murder, which he denied. Cortés then brashly proposed that in order to prove his innocence Moctezuma should transfer his residence to the palace occupied by the Spaniards. Astonishingly, the king agreed. Why Moctezuma surrendered himself is an abiding puzzle. "Now that I am an old man," writes Bernal Díaz, "I often entertain myself with calling to mind the heroical deeds, till they are as fresh as the events of yesterday. I think of the seizure of the Indian monarch, his confinement in irons, the execution of his officers, till all these things seem actually passing before me. And, as I ponder on our exploits, I feel that it was not ourselves that performed them, but that it was the providence of God which guided us. Much food is there here for meditation!"

There is another explanation — it was not so much the Christian God that triumphed as the Indian gods that failed their people. "Why did Moctezuma give up?" asks the Mexican poet Octavio Paz. "Why was he so fascinated by the Spaniards that he experienced a vertigo which it is no exaggeration to call sacred — the lucid vertigo of the suicide on the brink of the abyss? The gods had abandoned him. The great betrayal with which the history of Mexico begins was not committed by Tlaxcalans or by Moctezuma and his group; it was committed by the gods. No other people

The Aztec obsidian sacrificial knife above, left, was used
to cut out the hearts of the sun god's victims. The handle
represents a couchant eagle knight, or member of an
Aztec chivalric order. Above is the crowning of
Moctezuma, drawn for the Spanish historian Diego
Durán by a native artist.

have ever felt so completely helpless as the Aztec nation felt at the appearance of the omens, prophecies and warnings that announced its fall. . . . The mere presence of the Spaniards caused a split in Aztec society, a split corresponding to the dualism of their gods, their religious system and their castes."

In a literal way, Aztec religion helped doom the Aztec empire because the practice of human sacrifice was a serious military liability. Not only did the continuing need for victims make the Aztecs highly unpopular with their unfortunate neighbors, but the need to feed the altars did much to nullify Aztec prowess on the battlefield. Instead of trying to kill, the Aztecs sought to capture the Spaniards alive. At one crucial point, Cortés himself actually fell into Aztec hands during a battle; he managed to escape because his opponents were so intent on taking him alive. In a sense, Moctezuma was beaten before the war began; he and his people were immobilized by fatalism and by the peculiar demands of their religion. The emperor moved like a victim to the altar, all but inviting the final Aztec sacrifice. Cortés simply obliged him.

But the capture of Moctezuma was only an episode in an unfinished drama. News of Cortés's exploits had by now reached Cuba, and the envious Velázquez was almost apoplectic; he dispatched an army to punish his insubordinate captain. The commander of the punitive force was Pánfilo de Narváez, a soldier of some ability but with nothing of the craftiness of Cortés. By degrees, Narváez retraced the steps of Cortés, bringing his force to Cempoala, where it encamped. When word of the army's appearance reached Tenochtitlán, Cortés left the Aztec capital, gathered up his garrisons at Cholula

Two other scenes from the Diego Durán history depict Cortés receiving a beaded necklace from the Tlaxcalans, a sign of friendship or perhaps a token of the Spanish-Tlaxcalan alliance (top), and Pedro de Alvarado and his men blockaded in the palace (bottom). The massacre that Alvarado permitted in Cortés's absence resulted in the Indian uprising that led to the retreat from Tenochtitlán known as the Noche Triste.

and Tlaxcala, and prepared to wage battle with Narváez. In the war between Spaniard and Spaniard, Cortés easily won, partly by converting his rival's emissaries to his own cause with the help of Aztec gold and partly by outmaneuvering Narváez in a brief but decisive engagement.

During the absence of Cortés from the Mexican capital, the acting Spanish commander was Pedro de Alvarado, of whom Bernal Díaz says: "He had a merry, smiling face, and a very amorous glance. The Indians nicknamed him *Tonatio,* that is, the Sun, he was such a brilliant figure. He was lissom, a good rider, and above all of frank and open conversation. His clothes were always well-groomed and costly; round his neck he wore a golden chain, and a diamond ring on his fingers." Alvarado was also reckless and volatile.

A delegation of Aztec priests had asked permission to conduct a religious ceremony in the main plaza, and Alvarado gave his consent on condition that all the chiefs would come unarmed and that there would be no human sacrifices. Hundreds of Aztec nobles gathered on the appointed day, each wearing a magnificent feathered costume, when, without warning, the Spaniards fell upon the assemblage and slaughtered every Aztec chief. Why Pedro de Alvarado permitted this massacre is still unclear, but the result was to enrage a hitherto docile people, who now disavowed the captive Moctezuma and named his brother Cuitláhuac as emperor. In the uprising that followed, the Spaniards were blockaded in the palace in which they held Moctezuma a prisoner.

At this point Cortés, who had added Narváez's soldiers to his small force, rejoined his comrades. The Spanish captain saw that the situation was desperate, and induced the captive Moctezuma to mount the battlements and plead with his people. While trying to speak, Moctezuma was ignominiously stoned to death, his reign ending on June 30, 1520. The only other course, Cortés adjudged, was retreat, and what the Spaniards later called the *Noche Triste,* the "Sad Night," commenced. Before the breakout, the commander spread the Aztec treasure on the ground, saying: "Take what you will of it. But beware not to overload yourself." His own veterans heeded his advice, but Narváez's unseasoned troops greedily weighted themselves down with treasure, and many were killed as they tried to escape over the perilous causeways leading to the mainland.

On July 2, when the *Noche Triste* had passed, the retreating Spaniards found that they had lost a third of their force, all of their cannon, and most of their horses. About a fourth of their Tlaxcalan allies had perished. By arduous degrees, the Spaniards fought their way back towards the safe sanctuary of Tlaxcala, and it was during this retreat that Cortés and his men first saw the pyramids of Teotihuacán; one need not wonder that in his subsequent dispatch to his king, Cortés failed to make note of the discovery. On July 8, 1520, the remnants of the army found itself in a valley encircled by as many as 200,000 shouting Aztecs. In what was the supreme test of Spanish valor, the conquistadors burst through this armed sea, led by the mounted Cortés, who, in a providential incident, managed to single out and kill the Aztec commander. Cortés, though wounded, seized the fallen Aztec commander's staff with its golden banner. As he flourished

it, the Aztecs retreated before him, opening a passage of escape.

The rest is epilogue. Once back in the Tlaxcalan capital, the Spaniards nursed their wounds and prepared for a fresh attack on Tenochtitlán. With the help of reinforcements, Cortés supervised the construction of thirteen brigantines for use in the assault, which began in the spring of 1521. By that time the Spanish captain had assembled an army that included 75,000 Indians, 86 horsemen, 118 crossbowmen and musketeers, and about 700 foot soldiers. For their part, the Aztecs had chosen a new ruler, the young Cuauhtémoc, to succeed the fallen Cuitláhuac, who had died of smallpox, an insidious, additional Spanish ally. The final siege took three months, and at every point was fiercely fought, but the combination of superior Spanish military technology and the mass of Indian allies proved too much for the Aztecs. The last battle, in which Cuauhtémoc was captured, took place at Tlaltelolco, the city adjoining Tenochtitlán. The battlefield is now the site of the Mexican Ministry of Foreign Affairs and the Plaza of the Three Cultures. A large plaque near the remains of an Aztec temple bears these words: "The 13th of August of 1521, heroically defended by Cuauhtémoc, Tlaltelolco fell under the power of Hernan Cortés. It was not a triumph, not a defeat, it was the painful birth of the mixed race that is the Mexico of today."

After the Conquest, Bernal Díaz described what the Spaniards saw in the fallen city: "We found the houses full of corpses, and some poor Mexicans still in them who could not move away. Their excretions were the sort of filth that thin swine pass which have been fed nothing but grass. The city looked as if it had been ploughed up. The roots of any edible greenery had been dug out, boiled and eaten, and they had even cooked the bark of some of the trees. . . ."

It is to the credit of Cortés that after this calamity he applied himself to building a new political structure, which, if it was based on Indian servitude, at least had the merit of stability. (By contrast, after the conquest of Peru by Pizarro, there was a generation of civil war among the Spaniards, creating a climate of lawlessness that left its mark for years thereafter.) For three years Cortés was virtually king of Mexico, but his power aroused envy in the Spanish court and he was later displaced by a royal viceroy and given a splendid title — that of marquis of the Valley of Oaxaca — but little authority in the country he had conquered. At one point, he was forbidden to enter Mexico City, so fearful were the authorities that he intended mischief. When he sought to appeal directly to Charles V to live out his days not as a vagrant but as an honored servant of the king, he was dismissed as a tedious supplicant. He died, in solitary bitterness, while in Seville on December 2, 1547. He was sixty-three years old.

In a spacious paragraph, Prescott says of Cortés and his Conquest:

Whatever may be thought of the Conquest in a moral view, regarded as a military achievement it must fill us with astonishment. That a handful of adventurers, indifferently armed and equipped, should have landed on the shores of a powerful empire inhabited by a fierce and warlike race, and, in defiance of the reiterated prohibitions of its sovereign, should have forced their way into the interior; — that they should have

The effect of the conquistadors on the Indians is vividly shown in this 1540 drawing. Although they were, in Prescott's words, "indifferently armed and equipped," the Spaniards often had only to appear to cause entire villages of people to pack whatever of their belongings they could and flee in panic.

done this, without knowledge of the language or of the land, without chart or compass to guide them, without any idea of the difficulties they were to encounter, totally uncertain whether the next step might bring them on a hostile nation, or on a desert, feeling their way along in the dark, as it were; — that, though nearly overwhelmed by their first encounter with the inhabitants, they should have still pressed on to the capital of the empire, and having reached it, thrown themselves unhesitatingly in the midst of their enemies; . . . — that they should have seized the monarch, have executed his ministers before the eyes of his subjects, and, when driven forth with ruin from the gates, have gathered their scattered wreck together, and, after a system of operations, pursued with consummate policy and daring, have succeeded in overturning the capital, and establishing their sway over the country; — that all this should have been effected by a mere handful of indigent adventurers, is a fact little short of miraculous, — too startling for the probabilities demanded by fiction, and without parallel in the pages of history.

This post-Hispanic map of Teotihuacán shows the Avenue of the Dead running along the bottom with the Pyramid of the Moon at far left. Almost bisecting the avenue, with a small footprint to its right, is the Pyramid of the Sun. Farther to the

This frescoed ceremonial vessel with a tripod base is typical of Teotihuacán ceramics when that culture was at its peak, sometime between A.D. 400–700. Many such vessels had covers and were painted with the same designs and motifs that are found on the wall frescoes of the city. The cylindrical shape together with the three legs mark this as unmistakably of Teotihuacán origin.

every aspect of Spanish life before putting a word on paper. He taught himself to write with an ivory stylus on carbon paper, using a device known as a noctograph. His manuscript was then copied by his secretary in a hand large enough for the author to read. His first book took twelve years, and when it was finished he turned to a fresh subject — the conquest of Mexico.

Again, he prepared himself as if for battle. Four copyists in Madrid collected material for him in forgotten archives, sending him eight thousand sheets of precious manuscript, including material no other historian had seen. Friends in Mexico sent him books and papers on the Aztecs, and one of his valued informants was the Scottish wife of the Spanish envoy, Fanny Calderón de la Barca, who mailed him descriptions of the flora and landscape of Mexico, so that his history could evoke the very scent and shape of a country he never visited. Then, as a matter of protocol, he wrote to his only possible rival, Washington Irving, asking consent to go ahead. It was reluctantly given. ("I doubt," Irving later told a friend, "whether Prescott was aware that I gave him my bread.")

This was in 1839. By chance, in that same year another resourceful North American was setting sail into the Mesoamerican past. He was John Lloyd Stephens, also trained in law and like Prescott a man with an easy and winning manner; but whereas the Bostonian carried the world into his darkened study on Beacon Street, the New Yorker traveled everywhere to see for himself. In October, Stephens boarded the British brig *Mary Ann* bound for Central America, where he planned a quest for Maya ruins, which were then known only by rumor or the sketchiest of reports. His

companion was the English artist Frederick Catherwood, and in two epochal trips the pair of them were to lay the groundwork for American archaeology.

A circuitous route led Stephens to the Maya. After being admitted to the New York bar, he made a tour of Europe in 1834–36, partly for reasons of health, visiting England, France, Italy, Greece, Turkey, Russia, and Poland. Almost by accident, he became a writer; his chatty letters home were published, without his intending it, as magazine articles, and these he later shaped into a successful book. He had a light style, unpretentious and graceful, and showed a marked sagacity. While in Russia, the American meditatively wrote: "We are both young, and both marching with gigantic strides to greatness, yet we move by different roads; the whole face of the country, from the new city, Odessa, on the borders of the Black Sea, to the steppes of Siberia, shows a different order of government and a different constitution of society. With us a few individuals cut down the trees of a forest . . . and, by degrees, the little settlement becomes a large city. But here a gigantic government, endowed with almost creative powers, says '*Let there be a city.*'"

This travel book was coupled with another chronicling Stephens's ventures into Egypt, Arabia, and the Holy Land, where he became the first American to visit the magically desolate rose-red city of Petra, in Jordan. On his way back, Stephens stopped in London and met Frederick Catherwood, an artist of considerable talent who had sketched the ruins of the Middle East and who had fashioned a panorama of Jerusalem. The American urged the English artist to come to New York and exhibit his panorama, and Catherwood

Frederick Catherwood, with John Lloyd Stephens, was the modern rediscoverer of many Maya sites, among them Uxmal. On the opposite page is a detail from the Governor's Palace at Uxmal drawn by him and showing the combination of relief and mosaic that covered the façade of that building.
  Overleaf:
Catherwood's view of Palenque permits us to see how it looked after some — but not all — of the dense foliage that had obscured it for so many centuries had been removed. The palace complex (left) shows the remarkably intact tower, the roof of which has since been restored as shown in the photograph on pages 68–69.

agreed to the idea. On his return to New York, Stephens became immersed in politics — he was an ardent supporter of Andrew Jackson — and found himself a literary celebrity. The young Herman Melville long remembered that he once saw Stephens, "that wonderful Arabian Traveller," in church. ("See what big eyes he has," whispered Melville's aunt. "They got so big because when he was almost dead with famishing in the desert, he all at once caught sight of a date tree, with ripe fruit hanging on it.")

In 1837, after his book of Arabian travels was published, Stephens was browsing in a New York bookshop when the proprietor, one John R. Bartlett, asked why he didn't undertake an exploration of the Yucatán and Central America "where there are numerous objects of interest in ruined cities." Bartlett showed Stephens a book on the Yucatán with exotic pictures of the Maya site of Palenque, and the author was instantly interested. He invited Catherwood to join him, signed a contract with a publisher, and then somehow persuaded the Jacksonian administration of Martin Van Buren to appoint him as United States envoy to a newly established Central American confederation.

Stephens thus arrived in Belize, British Honduras, as an accredited diplomat — complete with a silver-buttoned blue uniform — as well as an explorer. He was then thirty-four years old. In the weird adventures that followed, Stephens had more luck in finding Maya ruins than in locating the ephemeral confederation, which burst apart just as he arrived. The writer and the artist first headed for the site of Copán, in Honduras, and came upon a magnificent Classic Maya city whose existence was hardly known to the rest of the

world. The artist sketched the ruins, while the author — in one of the unique transactions in the annals of archaeology — negotiated the purchase of Copán, with the idea of bringing back to New York some of the remarkable carvings he saw there. As Stephens described the transaction: "The reader is perhaps curious to know how old cities sell in Central America. Like other articles of trade, they are regulated by the quantity on the market and the demand; but . . . at that time were dull of sale. I paid $50 for Copán. There was never any difficulty about the price. I offered the sum for which Don José thought me a fool; if I had offered more, he would probably have considered me something worse."

After exploring Copán, Stephens and Catherwood went on to Guatemala City, met with various rebels and revolutionaries, and then pressed on to the Yucatán Peninsula in pursuit of more Maya ruins. They visited Palenque and Uxmal, making the first thorough survey of each great Maya site, and then proceeded back to New York, where, in a remarkably short time, a manuscript was completed. Stephens's *Incidents of Travel in Central America, Chiapas, and Yucatán* was published in 1841, in two thick volumes abundantly illustrated by Catherwood. The book was an immediate success, and among its first readers was W. H. Prescott, who wrote to Stephens: "You have made a tour over a most interesting ground, the very forum of American ruins, none of which has been given to the public. . . . Your opinion as to the comparatively modern dates of these remains agrees entirely with the conclusions I had come to from much more inadequate sources of information. . . ."

It is a testament to the shrewdness of Stephens that he dismissed as poppycock farfetched notions about the supposedly ancient date and alien origin of Maya civilization. As he wrote of the Maya cities: "They are different from the works of any other known people, of a new order, and entirely and absolutely anomalous: they stand alone." In further witness to his perspicacity, Stephens decided that one trip was not enough, and that he and Catherwood should go back for a second look. In 1841, the pair returned, confining their explorations this time to the Yucatán, where they visited no less than forty-four Maya sites, most of them unknown to the world, including the enormous ruin of Chichén Itzá. By this time, Stephens was no longer an amateur but was a serious Mayanist, and the resulting book, *Incidents of Travel in Yucatán,* was solider and more demanding than its predecessor. Considering that most of what Stephens and Catherwood saw was wholly new, the accuracy of the author's judgments and of the artist's drawings was little short of miraculous. Prescott was once more among the earliest readers, and he pronounced Stephens's second book "better than its brother."

It happened that Prescott's own monumental *History of the Conquest of Mexico* was published the same year, 1843, and Stephens was able to return the compliment. He called the *History* "the best book that was ever issued from the American press," adding, "Cortez is *used up*. No one will ever mount him again and your names will go down together til octavos are swallowed up by cheap literature." There was more than mutual gallantry in this pleasant exchange, because scholarship has certified the verdicts — Pres-

cott's volume on Mexico after more than a century remains unchallenged, the Everest in its field, while Stephens's reputation has grown steadily with the years. These two North Americans, so oddly unlike, together began the overdue rediscovery of the ancient past of their own continent. (Prescott went on to write *History of the Conquest of Peru,* and Stephens in 1848 helped organize the building of a railroad across Panama — while on the isthmus, he contracted a tropical disease which later caused his premature death, in 1852, in New York.)

Among the Maya achievements that especially impressed Stephens was the strange script that he found inscribed on the limestone stelae erected in plazas facing pyramids and temples. He wrote: "I cannot help believing that the tablets of hieroglyphics will yet be read." His hope seemed within easy fulfillment in 1863, when a long-lost key to the glyphs was found in a library in Madrid. The key was in a manuscript by Diego de Landa, bishop of Yucatán, who in the 1560's had located Indians still able to read hieroglyphics. After getting a translation for calendrical words, the bishop thought it would be relatively easy to correlate the Latin alphabet with Maya hieroglyphics. But many of the glyphs were symbols for words; thus, when the prelate asked for the sign for the letter "b" he got the word in Mayan for "road" or "journey," which has the same sound. Thus many hieroglyphs were left unexplained, and Landa's key turned out to be less than a Rosetta stone; even after more than a century of intensive international research, the hieroglyphs can be only partly read.

Nevertheless, Landa's manuscript helped open a

Maya stelae are stone monuments that record the relevant dates of Maya history (this one is inscribed with the equivalent of A.D. 766) as well as astronomical data. Quiriguá, where this stele was found, contained tablets and texts constituting, in Jacques Soustelle's words, "a kind of hymn to eternity," with calculations that cover a period of four hundred million years.

path into the thicket. In the appendix of his second book of *Incidents*, Stephens had included an invaluable account of Maya notation, which explained how the bars and dots stood for fives and digits; the account also gave the names of the various days and months of the Maya calendar. Using this information, a German librarian, Ernest Försterman, was able to identify the sign used for zero and to show that Maya arithmetic was similar to our own, except that it was based on units of twenty rather than ten. Försterman turned to the inscriptions of Copán, which Catherwood had drawn with such loving accuracy. By employing Landa's calendrical key, the Dresden scholar was able to read, in 1894, the dates on the stelae.

These dates were hardly a simple matter to unravel since the Maya, like other Mesoamerican peoples, used two interlocking calendars. There was a sacred year of 260 days, which was not marked off into months; each day was given one of twenty day names and was prefixed by a number, and it was this calendar which determined birthdays and patron gods (see chart, page 83). At the same time, there was a civil year composed of 365 days and divided into 18 months of 20 days each, plus a closing month of five days. Every fifty-two years the first days of the sacred and civil calendars would coincide. This fifty-two-year cycle was known as the Calendar Round; it was regarded in somewhat the fashion that we regard centuries. (Maya astronomers were of course aware that there was an extra quarter day each year, and they made corrective counts periodically to bring the calendar year into harmony with the solar year.) Still another system was used on dated inscriptions, which would begin with an Initial Series, or Long Count, reaching back to an arbitrary starting point, just as the Western calendar begins with the birth of Christ. From this starting point, time would be parceled into units of baktuns (144,000 days), katuns (7,200 days), tuns (360 days), uinals (20 days), and the kin (1 day). In the Maya system, the starting point reaches back more than three thousand years and may represent a priestly approximation rather than a record of a specific event.

Thanks to Försterman, the inscribed dates could be deciphered, but a further problem was to determine the correlation between the Maya Long Count and the Western calendar. The solution was found by an improbable amateur — Joseph Goodman, a mining tycoon and former newspaper publisher in Nevada and California, who has a niche in literary history as the first employer of Mark Twain. Goodman turned to the glyphs as a hobby, and in 1905 propounded a correlation that is generally accepted today and has proved consistent with carbon-14 dates of inscribed wooden Maya lintels.

In 1960, another major breakthrough was made by the Harvard scholar Tatiana Proskouriakoff, who noticed that the dates on one group of stelae at the site of Piedras Negras, in Guatemala, did not cover a span longer than a human life. Pursuing this insight, Miss Proskouriakoff was able to identify the symbols for specific rulers; apparently, two glyphs — known as the "upended frog" and the "toothache" glyphs — were like bookends around historical information. It thus became clear that actual events were described on the stelae, and that the final decipherment of Maya hieroglyphics may yet yield clues as to the mysterious collapse of Classic Maya civilization. (It must be sadly noted that scholars are in a race with looters, who have been devastating unguarded Maya sites to obtain carvings for the international art market.)

While some scholars were digging in libraries, others were excavating the Mexican earth, among them Manuel Gamio, a pioneer Mexican archaeologist. In 1910, at a site near Mexico City, Gamio cut into layers of refuse which, while they yielded no great works of art, turned up something more precious still — a stratified record of occupation levels covering a period of 1,400 years. At the deepest level were simple Preclassic clay figurines, then pottery in a style found at Teotihuacán and finally, at the top, sherds from the Aztec period. This first stratigraphic dig in Mexico made possible the compilation of a comparative chronology and pointed the way to the more rigorous techniques of present-day excavations.

For the first time, too, Mexican scholars began a systematic study of Teotihuacán on a major scale. The initial work started in 1905 and was directed by Leopoldo Batres. Batres was under pressure to restore the Pyramid of the Sun in time for celebrations of the centenary of Mexican independence in 1910, and in his zeal he mangled the monument, giving the pyramid five intermediary platforms instead of the archaeologically correct four. During the reconstruction, Teotihuacán began to attract the more venturesome foreign tourists. A classic early guidebook, T. Philip Terry's *Mexico*, published in 1909, advises visitors to obtain an official letter of introduction before taking a train to the village of San Juan Teotihuacán. At the station, "a species of buckboard is usually to be

The freestyle whimsy and pure caprice that the craftsmen of Teotihuacán indulged in from time to time are nowhere better demonstrated than in this pot, shaped like a bird with the beak of a quetzal and the body, apparently, of a turkey. When it was discovered, its excavators dubbed it the "crazy duck." Found at Teotihuacán, it dates from A.D. 250–375, or just before the apogee of that culture.

This is how Teotihuacán looked in 1895 — compare it with the present-day picture shown on pages 18–19. In this view, the Pyramid of the Sun is the large mound at left, the Avenue of the Dead has been narrowed to a path that bisects the picture, and the compound that stands in front of the Pyramid of the Moon, from which this photograph was also taken, is overgrown with scrub.

found" that will take tourists to the pyramids for fifty centavos. Terry continues:

> To those who bring the proper letters a local guide is usually furnished by the inspector. A little *meson* in the village provides indifferent food at a low price. A score or more Indian girls, with rich brown faces and snapping black eyes, await the traveller's arrival, and usually succeed in wheedling him into purchasing a clay mask, a bit of obsidian or nephrite, or a very friable idol of doubtful paternity. Many of the alleged antiques offered for sale near the ruins are spurious.

A great deal has changed — the tourist now reaches Teotihuacán on a toll superhighway, no letters of introduction are needed, and there is a luxury restaurant facing the ruins — but the same alleged antiques are still vended by the same persuasive youngsters.

In 1910, as Batres finished his labors at the Pyramid of the Sun, a political event occurred that was to affect every aspect of Mexican life, including archaeology. Since 1876, the republic had been ruled by the gifted but despotic General Porfirio Díaz, who was running for his eighth term in 1910. To the surprise of everyone — including Díaz himself — the reformer Francisco Madero won the election. The aged Díaz at first refused to resign but then fled the country as a popular rebellion began to flame. It was not a traditional factional struggle (as Díaz believed) but instead a true revolution, the first of its kind in the twentieth century.

The Mexican Revolution is as many-colored and complex as a mural by Diego Rivera or José Clemente Orozco. "Our movement was distinguished by a lack of any previous ideological system and by a hunger for

130

land," writes Octavio Paz. The Mexican peasants supported the revolution not merely to achieve better living conditions, but also to recover lands that had been taken during the colonial period and in the nineteenth century. But on another level, the revolution was much more than an agrarian revolt — it involved, too, an effort to recapture a golden age, a time free of alien contamination. As Paz continues: "This explains why the character of the movement is both desperate and redemptive. If these words still have any meaning for us after so many repetitions, they mean that the people refuse all outside help, every imported scheme, every idea lacking some profound relationship to their intimate feelings, and that instead they turn to themselves." And to their past.

After the revolution, archaeology ceased to be a concern solely of specialists but became instead an integral part of public policy. Díaz had scorned the Indianism of his country and imported architects from France to design glittering opera houses and public buildings. This is no longer the case in Mexico, where every effort is made to seek out indigenous motifs — as in the capital's new subway stations or as in the stadium and library of the University of Mexico. In all of this, Teotihuacán has taken on a new identity; it is no longer a curiosity but a symbol.

Even while the battles between Mexican revolutionaries were being waged, major explorations were undertaken at Teotihuacán under the able guidance of Manuel Gamio in 1917. Gamio's work can be seen at the Temple of Quetzalcoatl and in the Citadel, where his restorations were far more skillful than the heavy-handed efforts of Batres at the Pyramid of the Sun. With Gamio, a new era of scientific inquiry began at Teotihuacán. From 1932 to 1935, the Swedish archaeologist Sigvald Linné unearthed the first palace residences at Teotihuacán, which turned out to be larger than anyone had expected. At one complex, Linné uncovered a conglomeration of 175 rooms built around a network of corridors and encompassing a total of 4,000 square yards. In inner courts, he found not only spacious basins for water but also the finely polished stone plugs used to stop the drains, some of them still in situ. "We can almost be certain that these houses had no upper storeys," Linné reported, "and that the flat roofs sloped inwards towards the inner court where the water collected." Two of the houses he discovered were suggestive of hotels rather than permanently inhabited dwellings, confirming that Teotihuacán was a place of pilgrimage frequented by thousands of visitors. As a result of the Swedish scholar's work, the urban nature of Teotihuacán for the first time became apparent.

Further evidence of Teotihuacán's urban amenities came to light when the French-born Mexican archaeologist Laurette Séjourné dug into a bean field in 1955–57 and found beneath it the ruins of a palace covering about five thousand square yards. The Palace of Zacuala had lavish murals, some of them depicting gods whose images appeared at a much later date in Tenochtitlán. To Señora Séjourné, the finds appeared to corroborate her controversial thesis that Teotihuacán was the cradle of Nahuatl civilization and that its benign deities were later displaced by the bloody war gods of the Aztecs. In a further excavation, at the Palace of Tetitla, carried out in 1963, Señora

133

Séjourné unearthed still more fascinating mural art, including a painting of a ravenous tiger limned in bold colors and strong brushstrokes unusual in Teotihuacano art.

But the greatest single campaign carried out at the pyramid city was made possible by the enlightened political intervention of a Mexican president, Adolfo López Mateos. All archaeological work sponsored by the government is under the supervision of the National Institute of Anthropology and History, whose director in 1960 was the late Eusebio Dávalos Hurtado. It had long been his hope that the dozens of buried temples bounding Teotihuacán's Avenue of the Dead could one day be excavated and restored, thereby giving a visitor a more vivid sense of the city's past splendor. Dr. Dávalos, to his delight, found that the recently elected López Mateos was receptive; funds were duly appropriated for a major, two-year campaign.

The Avenue of the Dead was finally cleared of debris, and the many ceremonial platforms adjoining it were restored to their ancient shape. The city was divided into seven zones, and in each the soil was meticulously sifted for evidence about its inhabitants. A score of archaeologists directed the spades of six hundred workmen, and in swift order the plaza in front of the Pyramid of the Moon was cleared and refurbished and the labyrinthian Butterfly Palace came to light. As a consequence, it no longer requires a robust feat of imagination to glimpse the past magnificence of Teotihuacán. At the same time, President López Mateos authorized the construction of the new National Museum of Anthropology, which was completed in twenty months. In 1964, the Mexican president in a single week dedicated the new museum, opened the superhighway leading to the pyramids of Teotihuacán, and toured the restored site. Among the foreign visitors during the gala week was Sir Philip Hendy, then director of the National Gallery of Art in London; he commented in *The Times*: "In museography Mexico is now ahead of the United States by perhaps a generation, of the United Kingdom perhaps by a century."

Comments about the museum and the restoration of Teotihuacán are not always so flattering. Archaeologists complain that scholarship has been subordinated to theatricality — that the restoration of the pyramids is too flashy, and that the money could have been better spent on other sites. There is some validity to the reproach, but it ignores the needs of Mexico and the realities of tourism. It also ignores the special magic of the site. "Solitude and communion, individuality and universality," writes Octavio Paz, "are still the extremes that devour every Mexican." These extremes take on a tangible reality at Teotihuacán, where the visitor is at once overwhelmed by isolation and yet caught up in a collective sweep of humanity just as overwhelming. Teotihuacán is that rare thing among the great monuments of the world, a place where the metaphysically minded and the literal minded can glean their separate satisfactions. Mexicans have every right to be proud of Teotihuacán, and foreign visitors have every reason to be impressed. By making America's first city accessible to everyone, and by striving to restore its dwellings and its templed vistas, the Mexicans have earned general thanks. They are making Teotihuacán — and the Indian civilization it represents — part of the common property of all mankind.

ANCIENT MEXICO IN LITERATURE

According to Aztec myth, the capital city of Tenochtitlán was founded on a site where the Aztecs saw an eagle devouring its prey atop a cactus. The event was commemorated in a section of the Codex Mendoza (opposite), a 1541 document prepared by the Indians at Spanish behest. On the following pages of Ancient Mexico in Literature *appear illustrations from the Codex Florentine of Bernardino de Sahagún.*

THE CONQUERORS

The narratives of the Spanish conquerors contain not only detailed accounts of the Conquest, but also valuable descriptions of the pre-Columbian world. The great Aztec capital of Tenochtitlán, which did not surrender until totally anni- hilated, is known only through their descriptions. Probably the most famous of these narratives are the letters Hernán Cortés wrote to his emperor, Charles V. In Cortés's portrayal of Tenochtitlán, we sense his awe and wonder. But the Spanish conqueror of Mexico was impressed only by the material wealth of the Aztecs — the markets brimming with gold, silver, precious jewels, bright feathers, and exotic foods, the magnificent temples, and Moctezuma's luxurious palaces. The civilization the Aztecs had evolved meant nothing to him.

Most Powerful Lord, in order to give an account to Your Royal Excellency of the magnificence, the strange and marvelous things of this great city of Temixtitan and of the dominion and wealth of this Mutezuma, its ruler, and of the rites and customs of the people, and of the order there is in the government of the capital as well as in the other cities of Mutezuma's do- minions, I would need much time and many expert narrators. I cannot describe one hundredth part of all the things which could be mentioned, but, as best I can, I will describe some of those I have seen which . . . will, I well know, be so remarkable as not to be believed, for we who saw them with our own eyes could not grasp them with our understanding. . . .

This great city of Temixtitan is built on the salt lake, and no matter by what road you travel there are two leagues from the main body of the city to the mainland. There are four artificial causeways leading to it, and each is as wide as two cavalry lances. The city itself is as big as Seville or Córdoba. The main streets are very wide and very straight; some of these are on the land, but the rest and all the smaller ones are half on land, half canals where they paddle their canoes. All the streets have openings in places so that the water may pass from one canal to another. Over all these openings, and some of them are very wide, there are bridges made of long and wide beams joined together very firmly and so well made that on some of them ten horsemen may ride abreast. . . .

This city has many squares where trading is done and markets are held con- tinuously. There is also one square twice as big as that of Salamanca, with arcades all around, where more than sixty thousand people come each day to buy and sell, and where every kind of merchandise produced in these lands is found; provisions as well as ornaments of gold and silver, lead, brass, copper, tin, stones, shells, bones, and feathers. They also sell lime, hewn and unhewn stone, adobe bricks, tiles, and cut and uncut woods of various kinds. There is a street where they sell game and birds of every species found in this land: chickens, partridges and quails, wild ducks, flycatchers, widg- eons, turtledoves, pigeons, cane birds, parrots, eagles and eagle owls, fal- cons, sparrow hawks and kestrels, and they sell the skins of some of these birds of prey with their feathers, heads and claws. They sell rabbits and hares, and stags and small gelded dogs which they breed for eating.

There are streets of herbalists where all the medicinal herbs and roots found in the land are sold. There are shops like apothecaries', where they sell ready-made medicines as well as liquid ointments and plasters. There are shops like barbers' where they have their hair washed and shaved, and shops where they sell food and drink. There are also men like porters to carry loads. There is much firewood and charcoal, earthenware braziers and mats of various kinds like mattresses for beds, and other, finer ones, for seats and for covering rooms and hallways. There is every sort of vegetable, especially onions, leeks, garlic, common cress and watercress, borage, sorrel, teasels and artichokes; and there are many sorts of fruit, among which are cherries and plums like those in Spain.

They sell honey, wax, and a syrup made from maize canes, which is as sweet and syrupy as that made from the sugar cane. They also make syrup from a plant which in the islands is called *maguey,* which is much better than most syrups, and from this plant they also make sugar and wine, which they likewise sell. There are many sorts of spun cotton, in hanks of every color, and it seems like the silk market at Granada, except here there is a much greater quantity. They sell as many colors for painters as may be found in Spain and all of excellent hues. They sell deerskins, with and without the hair, and some are dyed white or in various colors. They sell much earthenware, which for the most part is very good; there are both large and small pitchers, jugs, pots, tiles, and many other sorts of vessel, all of good clay and most of them glazed and painted. They sell maize both as grain and as bread and it is better both in appearance and in taste than any found in the islands or on the mainland. They sell chicken and fish pies, and much fresh and salted fish, as well as raw and cooked fish. They sell hen and goose eggs, and eggs of all the other birds I have mentioned, in great number, and they sell *tortillas* made from eggs. . . .

There are, in all districts of this great city, many temples or houses for their idols. . . . Amongst these temples there is one, the principal one, whose great size and magnificence no human tongue could describe, for it is so large that within the precincts, which are surrounded by a very high wall, a town of some five hundred inhabitants could easily be built. All round inside this wall there are very elegant quarters with very large rooms and corridors where their priests live. There are as many as forty towers, all of which are so high that in the case of the largest there are fifty steps leading up to the main part of it; and the most important of these towers is higher than that of the cathedral of Seville. They are so well constructed in both their stone and woodwork that there can be none better in any place, for all the stonework inside the chapels where they keep their idols is in high relief, with figures and little houses, and the woodwork is likewise of relief and painted with monsters and other figures and designs. All these towers are burial places of chiefs, and the chapels therein are each dedicated to the idol which he venerated.

There are three rooms within this great temple for the principal idols, which are of remarkable size and stature and decorated with many designs and sculptures, both in stone and in wood. Within these rooms are other chapels, and the doors to them are very small. Inside there is no light whatsoever; there only some of the priests may enter, for inside are the sculptured figures of the idols, although, as I have said, there are also many outside.

The most important of these idols, and the ones in whom they have most faith, I had taken from their places and thrown down the steps; and I had those chapels where they were cleaned, for they were full of the blood of sacrifices; and I had images of Our Lady and of other saints put there, which caused Mutezuma and the other natives some sorrow. First they asked me not to do it, for when the communities learnt of it they would rise against me, for they believed that those idols gave them all their worldly goods, and that if they were allowed to be ill treated, they would become angry and give them nothing and take the fruit from the earth leaving the people to die of hunger. I made them understand through the interpreters how deceived they were in placing their trust in those idols which they had made with their hands from unclean things. They must know that there was only one God, Lord of all things, who had created heaven and earth and all else and who made all of us; and He was without beginning or end, and they must adore and worship only Him, not any other creature or thing. And I told them all I knew about this to dissuade them from their idolatry and bring them to the knowledge of God our Saviour. All of them, especially Mutezuma, replied that they had already told me how they were not natives of this land, and that as it was many years since their forefathers had come here, they well knew that they might have erred somewhat in what they believed, for they had left their native land so long ago; and as I had only recently arrived from there, I would better know the things they should believe, and should explain to them and make them understand, for they would do as I said was best. Mutezuma and many of the chieftains of the city were with me until the idols were removed, the chapel cleaned and the images set up, and I urged them not to sacrifice living creatures to the idols, as they were accustomed, for, as well as being most abhorrent to God, Your Sacred Majesty's laws forbade it and ordered that he who kills shall be killed. And from then on they ceased to do it, and in all the time I stayed in that city I did not see a living creature killed or sacrificed.

The figures of the idols in which these people believe are very much larger than the body of a big man. They are made of dough from all the seeds and vegetables which they eat, ground and mixed together, and bound with the blood of human hearts which those priests tear out while still beating. And also after they are made they offer them more hearts and anoint their faces with the blood. Everything has an idol dedicated to it, in the same manner as the pagans who in antiquity honored their gods. So they have an idol whose favor they ask in war and another for agriculture; and likewise for each thing they wish to be done well they have an idol which they honor and serve.

There are in the city many large and beautiful houses, and the reason for this is that all the chiefs of the land, who are Mutezuma's vassals, have houses in the city and live there for part of the year; and in addition there are many rich citizens who likewise have very good houses. All these houses have very large and very good rooms and also very pleasant gardens of various sorts of flowers both on the upper and lower floors.

Along one of the causeways to this great city run two aqueducts made of mortar. Each one is two paces wide and some six feet deep, and along one of them a stream of very good fresh water, as wide as a man's body, flows into the heart of the city and from this they all drink. The other, which is empty, is used when they wish to clean the first channel. Where the aqueducts cross the bridges, the water passes along some channels which are as wide as an ox; and so they serve the whole city.

Canoes paddle through all the streets selling the water; they take it from the aqueduct by placing the canoes beneath the bridges where those channels are, and on top there are men who fill the canoes and are paid for their work. . . . Every day, in all the markets and public places there are many workmen and craftsmen of every sort, waiting to be employed by the day. The people of this city are dressed with more elegance and are more courtly in their bearing than those of the other cities and provinces, and because Mutezuma and all those chieftains, his vassals, are always coming to the city, the people have more manners and politeness in all matters. Yet so as not to tire Your Highness with the description of the things of this city (although I would not complete it so briefly), I will say only that these people live almost like those in Spain, and in as much harmony and order as there, and considering that they are barbarous and so far from the knowledge of God and cut off from all civilized nations, it is truly remarkable to see what they have achieved in all things.

HERNAN CORTES
Letter to Charles V, 1520

Bernal Díaz del Castillo was born in Spain in 1492. His youth coincided with Spain's Golden Age; he was thoroughly imbued with the Renaissance optimism of that epoch and his imagination had been inflamed by Amadis of Gaul *and other romances of chivalry. These tales resembled authentic chronicles and consisted of the accounts of knightly heroes in search of strange and enchanted places, such as El Dorado and the Fountains of Youth. Díaz became one of Cortés's footsoldiers, and the spirited narrative he wrote on the Conquest has something of the quality of the romances of the day. This is particularly true of his description of the Aztec capital.*

During the morning, we arrived at a broad Causeway and continued our march towards Iztapalapa, and when we saw so many cities and villages built in the water and other great towns on dry land and that straight and level Causeway going towards Mexico, we were amazed and said that it was like the enchantments they tell of in the legend of Amadis, on account of the great towers and cues and buildings rising from the water, and all built of masonry. And some of our soldiers even asked whether the things that we saw were not a dream. It is not to be wondered at that I here write it down in this manner, for there is so much to think over that I do not know how to describe it, seeing things as we did that had never been heard of or seen before, not even dreamed about.

Thus, we arrived near Iztapalapa, to behold the splendour of the other Caciques who came out to meet us, who were the Lord of the town named Cuitlahuac, and the Lord of Culuacan, both of them near relations of Montezuma. And then when we entered the city of Iztapalapa, the appearance of the palaces in which they lodged us! How spacious and well built they were, of beautiful stone work and cedar wood, and the wood of other sweet scented trees, with great rooms and courts, wonderful to behold, covered with awnings of cotton cloth.

When we had looked well at all of this, we went to the orchard and garden, which was such a wonderful thing to see and walk in, that I was never tired of looking at the diversity of the trees, and noting the scent which each one had, and the paths full of roses and flowers, and the many fruit trees and native roses, and the pond of fresh water. There was another thing to observe, that great canoes were able to pass into the garden from the lake through an opening that had been made so that there was no need for their occupants to land. And all was cemented and very splendid with many kinds of stone [monuments] with pictures on them, which gave much to think about. Then the birds of many kinds and breeds which came into the pond. I say again that I stood looking at it and thought that never in the world would there be discovered other lands such as these, for at that time there was no Peru, nor any thought of it. Of all these wonders that I then beheld to-day all is overthrown and lost, nothing left standing.

BERNAL DIAZ DEL CASTILLO
The Discovery and Conquest of Mexico, 1517–21

The principal task of the Dominican and Franciscan friars who followed the conquistadors was, of course, conversion. But to achieve this end, it was essential for the missionaries to fully understand the indigenous culture. Fluent in Nahuatl, they used native informants and documents to record the legends and songs of the Aztecs. Because they did not wish to destroy the Indian culture, but only to evangelize it, the Spanish missionaries have left us with an important source of Aztec history. In the following passage, Fray Diego Durán relates the Aztec legend of the founding of Tenochtitlán.

The next day in the morning, the priest Cuauhtloquetzqui, anxious to impart the revelation from his god and to inform the people of what he had seen in dreams, ordered everyone to gather, men and women, old and young. When all had gathered he began to extol the great favors that they received each day from their god. He talked especially about the happy tidings that had just been revealed. The Aztecs had already seen that day in the spring white water snakes, frogs, fish, willows and junipers, all white.

Cuauhtloquetzqui declared that another no less wonderful thing had been disclosed to prove that this was the place chosen by their god for their shelter, where they could multiply and where the Aztec nation would excel, its greatness becoming renowned. He cried out:

"Know, my children, that last night Huitzilopochtli appeared to me. Remember, on our arrival in this valley, that we went to Chapultepec Hill where the god's nephew Copil was. Copil, having resolved on war against us, used his cunning and deceit to bring our enemies around us and to kill our captain, Huitzilihuitl. Our enemies drove us from that region, but Huitzilopochtli commanded us to kill Copil and this we did, taking out his heart. And standing in the place where he commanded, I threw the heart into the reeds; it fell upon a rock. According to the revelation of our god a prickly pear cactus has grown from this heart and become a tree so tall and luxuriant that a fine eagle rests there. Huitzilopochtli commands us to look for this place. When we discover it we shall be fortunate, for there we shall find our rest, our comfort and our grandeur. There our name will be praised and our Aztec nation made great. The might of our arms will be known and the courage of our brave hearts. With these we will conquer nations, near and distant, we will subdue towns and cities from sea to sea. We will become lords of gold and silver, of jewels and precious stones, of splendid feathers and of the insignia that distinguish lords and chieftains. We will rule over these peoples, their lands, their sons and daughters. They will serve us and be our subjects and tributaries.

"Our god orders us to call this place Tenochtitlan. There will be built the city that is to be queen of all others in the country. There we will receive other kings and nobles, who will recognize Tenochtitlan as the supreme capital. And so, my children, let us go among these marshes of reeds and rushes as our god has indicated. Everything he has promised us has come true!"

When the Aztecs heard what Cuauhtloquetzqui said to them, they humbled themselves before their deity. They gave thanks to the Lord of All Created Things, of the Day and the Night, Wind and Fire. Then, dividing into different groups, they went into the swamp, searching among the reeds.

Thus they returned to the clear, transparent spring they had seen the day before. Now the water rushed out in two streams, one red like blood, the other so blue and thick that it filled the people with awe. Having seen these mysterious things the Aztecs continued to seek the omen of the eagle. Wandering from one place to another, they soon discovered the prickly pear cactus. On it stood the eagle with his wings stretched out toward the rays of the sun, basking in their warmth and the freshness of the morning. In his talons he held a bird with very fine feathers, precious and shining. When the people saw the eagle they humbled themselves, making reverences almost as if the bird were a divine thing. The eagle, seeing them, bowed his head in their direction.

As the Aztecs observed this they realized that they had come to the end of their journey and they began to weep with contentment. In thanksgiving they said, "By what right do we deserve such good fortune? Who made us worthy of such grace? We have at last fulfilled our desires; we have found what we sought, our capital. Let thanks be given to the Lord of All Created Things, our god Huitzilopochtli!" They then marked the site and went to rest.

The next day the priest Cuauhtloquetzqui told the members of the company, "My children, it is only just that we be grateful to our god and that we thank him for all that he does for us. Let us go and make a small temple where our divinity can rest in the place of the prickly pear cactus. It cannot yet be of stone so let it be constructed of earth. For the present we can do no more." . . .

Although the wood and stone were not sufficient, the Aztecs began to build their temple. Little by little they filled in and consolidated the site for the city. They built foundations in the water by driving in stakes and throwing dirt and stone between the stakes. Thus they planned their city and founded it. They covered the outside of the little mud shrine with a coating of small cut stones, then plastered it with a lime finish. So, although it was small and humble, the home of their god acquired a pleasing appearance.

The night after the Aztecs had finished their god's temple, when an extensive part of the lake had been filled in and the foundations for their houses made, Huitzilopochtli spoke to his priests. "Tell the Aztec people that the principal men, each with his relatives and friends and allies, should divide the city into four main wards. The center of the city will be the house you have constructed for my resting place."

These wards are the ones that still exist in the city of Mexico. They are San Pablo, San Juan, Santa Mariá la Redonda, and San Sebastián.

FRAY DIEGO DURAN
The History of the Indies of New Spain, 1581

The narratives of the conquerors relate one side of the history of ancient Mexico; the documents of the conquered tell quite another. Writing in Nahuatl, the Aztec tongue, but using the Latin alphabet, Indian sources poignantly evoke a civilization lost forever. Each of the following documents describes the final capitulation of Tenochtitlán. The first, by Alva Ixtlilxochitl, himself a descendant of the Texcoco king and ally of Cortés, recreates the surrender of the last Aztec emperor. The last two, both anonymous elegies from collections of post-Conquest Aztec poems called, respectively, the Cantares Mexicanos *and* Unos Anales Historicos de la Nacion Mexicana, *capture the trauma of the Indians' defeat. The flower is a common Aztec symbol for man's brief and fleeting life on earth.*

On the day that Tenochtitlan was taken, the Spaniards committed some of the most brutal acts ever inflicted upon the unfortunate people of this land. The cries of the helpless women and children were heart-rending. The Tlaxcaltecas and the other enemies of the Aztecs revenged themselves pitilessly for old offenses and robbed them of everything they could find. Only Prince Ixtlilxochitl of Tezcoco, ally of Cortes, felt compassion for the Aztecs, because they were of his own homeland. He kept his followers from mistreating the women and children as cruelly as did Cortes. . . .

The anguish and bewilderment of our foes was pitiful to see. The warriors gathered on the rooftops and stared at the ruins of their city in a dazed silence, and the women and children and old men were all weeping. The lords and nobles crowded into the canoes with their king.

At a given signal, our forces attacked the enemy all at once. We pressed forward so swiftly that within a few hours we had totally defeated them. Our brigantines and canoes attacked their flotilla; they could not withstand us but scattered in every direction, with our forces pursuing them. Garcia de Olguin, who commanded one of the brigantines, was told by an Aztec prisoner that the canoe he was following was that of the king. He bore down on it and gradually caught up with it.

Cuauhtemoc, seeing that the enemy was overtaking him, ordered the boatman to turn the canoe toward our barkentine and prepare to attack it. He grasped his shield and *macana* and was determined to give battle. But when he realized that the enemy could overwhelm him with crossbows and muskets, he put down his arms and surrendered.

Garcia de Olguin brought him before Cortes, who received him with all the respect due to a king. Cuauhtemoc placed his hand on the Captain's dagger and said: "I have done everything in my power to save my kingdom from your hands. Since fortune has been against me, I now beg you to take my life. This would put an end to the kingship of Mexico, and it would be just and right, for you have already destroyed my city and killed my people." He spoke other grief-stricken words, which touched the heart of everyone who heard them.

Cortes consoled him and asked him to command his warriors to surrender. Cuauhtemoc immediately climbed onto a high tower and shouted to them to cease fighting, for everything had fallen to the enemy. Of the 300,000 warriors who had defended the city, 60,000 were left. When they heard their king, they laid down their arms and the nobles came forward to comfort him.

FERNANDO DE ALVA IXTLILXOCHITL
XII Relacion, ca. 1600

Nothing but flowers and songs of sorrow
are left in Mexico and Tlatelolco,
where once we saw warriors and wise men.

We know it is true
that we must perish,
for we are mortal men.
You, the Giver of Life,
you have ordained it.

We wander here and there
in our desolate poverty.
We are mortal men.
We have seen bloodshed and pain
where once we saw beauty and valor.

We are crushed to the ground;
we lie in ruins.
There is nothing but grief and suffering
in Mexico and Tlatelolco,
where once we saw beauty and valor.

Have you grown weary of your servants?
Are you angry with your servants,
O Giver of Life?

ANONYMOUS AZTEC POET
Cantares Mexicanos, 1523

Broken spears lie in the roads;
we have torn our hair in our grief.
The houses are roofless now, and their walls
are red with blood.

Worms are swarming in the streets and plazas,
and the walls are spattered with gore.
The water has turned red, as if it were dyed,
and when we drink it,
it has the taste of brine.

We have pounded our hands in despair
against the adobe walls,
for our inheritance, our city, is lost and dead.
The shields of our warriors were its defense,
but they could not save it.

We have chewed dry twigs and salt grasses;
we have filled our mouths with dust and bits of adobe;
we have eaten lizards, rats and worms.

ANONYMOUS AZTEC POET
Unos Anales Historicos de la Nacion Mexicana, 1528

145

Aldous Huxley is known as an essayist, novelist, short story writer, and — in his last years — mystic. His Beyond the Mexique Bay, *published in 1934, recounts the impressions he received while on a trip through Mexico, including this insight into the Spanish Conquest.*

The story of the Spanish conquest is true but incredible. That Tenochtitlan was taken, that Cortes marched from Mexico to Honduras, that Alvarado broke the power of the Quichés and Cakchiquels — these are facts, but facts so immoderately unlikely that I have never been able to believe them except on authority; reason and imagination withheld their assent. At Panajachel, I made an acquaintance who convinced me, for the first time, that everything in Prescott and Bernal Diaz had really happened. He was an old Spaniard who lived with an Indian wife and their family in a large rambling house by the lake, making his living as a taxidermist and dresser of skins. He was wonderfully expert at his job and had a first-hand knowledge of the birds, mammals and reptiles of the country. But it was not what he did or said that interested me most; it was what he was. As I watched him moving about the terrace of his house, a gaunt, bony figure, but active and powerful, his black beard aggressive in the wind, his nose like an eagle's, his eyes glittering, restless and fierce, I suddenly understood the how and the why of the Spanish conquest. The strength of the Indians is a strength of resistance, of passivity. Matched against these eager, violently active creatures from across the sea, they had no chance — no more chance than a rock against a sledge hammer. True, the Indian rock was a very large one, but the hammer, though small, was wielded with terrific force. Under its quick re-iterated blows, the strangely sculptured monolith of American civilization broke into fragments. The bits are still there, indestructible, and perhaps some day they may be fused together again into a shapely whole; meanwhile they merely testify, in their scattered nullity, to the amazing force behind the Spanish hammer.

The old taxidermist went into the house and returned a moment later with a large bucket full of a glutinous and stinking liquid.

"Look here," he said; and he drew out of this disgusting soup yards and yards of an enormous snakeskin. *"Qué bonito!"* he kept repeating, as he smoothed it out. "Like silk. Nobody here knows how to tan a snakeskin as well as I."

I nodded and made the appropriate noises. But it was not at the skin that I was looking; it was at the old man's hands. They were big hands, with fingers long, but square-tipped; hands that moved with a deft power, that reached out and closed with a quick, unhesitating rapacity; the hands of a *conquistador.*

He asked too much for the skin he finally sold us; but I did not grudge the money; for, along with two yards of beautiful serpent's leather, I had bought the key to Spanish-American history, and to me that was worth several times the extra dollar I had paid for my python.

ALDOUS HUXLEY
Beyond the Mexique Bay, 1934

D. H. Lawrence's view of the Spanish conquerors is in sharp contrast to Huxley's. Probably one of the greatest descriptive writers in English, Lawrence spent five years in Mexico and the American Southwest. The Plumed Serpent *reflects the profound emotions he himself felt among the American and Mexican Indians.*

Mexico! The great, precipitous, dry, savage country, with a handsome church in every landscape, rising as it were out of nothing. A revolution broken landscape, with lingering, tall, handsome churches whose domes are like inflations that are going to burst, and whose pinnacles and towers are like the trembling pagodas of an unreal race. Gorgeous churches waiting, above the huts and straw hovels of the natives, like ghosts to be dismissed.

And noble ruined haciendas, with ruined avenues approaching their broken splendour.

And the cities of Mexico, great and small, that the Spaniards conjured up out of nothing. Stones live and die with the spirit of the builders. And the spirit of Spaniards in Mexico dies, and the very stones in the building die. The natives drift into the centre of the plazas again, and in unspeakable empty weariness the Spanish buildings stand around, in a sort of dry exhaustion.

The conquered race! Cortes came with his iron heel and his iron will, a conqueror. But a conquered race, unless grafted with a new inspiration, slowly sucks the blood of the conquerors, in the silence of a strange night and the heaviness of a hopeless will. So that now, the race of the conquerors in Mexico is soft and boneless, children crying in helpless hopelessness.

Was it the dark negation of the continent?

Kate could not look at the stones of the National Museum in Mexico without depression and dread. Snakes coiled like excrement, snakes fanged and feathered beyond all dreams of dread. And that was all.

The ponderous pyramids of San Juan Teotihuacan, the House of Quetzalcoatl wreathed with the snake of all snakes, his huge fangs white and pure to-day as in the lost centuries when his makers were alive. He had not died. He is not so dead as the Spanish churches, this all-enwreathing dragon of the horror of Mexico.

Cholula, with its church where the altar was! And the same ponderousness, the same unspeakable sense of weight and downward pressure of the blunt pyramid. Down-sinking pressure and depression. And the great marketplace with its lingering dread and fascination.

Mitla under its hills, in the parched valley where a wind blows the dust and the dead souls of the vanished race in terrible gusts. The carved courts of Mitla, with a hard, sharp-angled, intricate fascination, but the fascination of fear and repellence. Hard, four-square, sharp-edged, cutting, zig-zagging Mitla, the continual blows of a stone axe. Without gentleness or grace or charm. Oh America, with your unspeakable hard lack of charm, what then is your final meaning! Is it forever the knife of sacrifice, as you put out your tongue at the world?

Charmless America! With your hard, vindictive beauty, are you waiting forever to smite death? Is the world your everlasting victim?

So long as it will let itself be victimised.

But yet! But yet! The gentle voices of the natives. The voices of the boys, like birds twittering among the trees of the plaza of Tehuacan! The soft touch, the gentleness. Was it the dark-fingered quietness of death, and the music of the presence of death in their voices?

She thought again of what Don Ramón had said to her.

"They pull you down! Mexico pulls you down, the people pull you down like a great weight! But it may be they pull you down as the earth's pull of gravitation does, that you can balance on your feet. Maybe they draw you down as the earth draws down the roots of a tree, so that it may be clinched deep in soil. Men are still part of the Tree of Life, and the roots go down to the centre of the earth. Loose leaves, and aeroplanes, blow away on the wind, in what they call freedom. But the Tree of Life has fixed, deep, gripping roots.

"It may be you need to be drawn down, down, till you send roots into the deep places again. Then you can send up the sap and the leaves back to the sky, later.

"And to me, the men in Mexico are like trees, forests that the white men felled in their coming. But the roots of the trees are deep and alive and forever sending up new shoots.

"And each new shoot that comes up overthrows a Spanish church or an American factory. And soon the dark forest will rise again, and shake the Spanish buildings from the face of America.

"All that matters to me are the roots that reach down beyond all destruction. The roots and the life are there. What else it needs is the word, for the forest to begin to rise again. And some man among men must speak the word."

The strange doom-like sound of the man's words! But in spite of the sense of doom on her heart, she would not go away yet. She would stay longer in Mexico.

D. H. LAWRENCE
The Plumed Serpent, 1926

The earliest description of Teotihuacán is contained in an official report written by Corregidor Don Francisco de Castañeda to Philip II in 1580. The statement that Moctezuma and his priests came to Teotihuacán every twenty days reveals that the ancient city continued to be an important religious center up until the time of the Spanish Conquest.

EARLY SEEKERS

In heathen times [the people of Teotihuacán] constituted a republic which recognized no authority but that of its natural lords who were [of the race] named Chichimecas, until Netzahualcoyotzin, lord of Texcoco, made war and tyrannized over the whole territory, killing sons of Tetzotzomoctzin, lord of Atzcapotzalco, to whom all rendered allegiance. After the death of Tetzotzomoctzin the said Netzahualcoyotzin made himself powerful by making an alliance with Montezuma, lord of Mexico. They divided between themselves the lands of the towns of Teotihuacan and Acolman. The inhabitants of Teotihuacan, in recognition of their overlordship, paid them as tribute, every eight days, some blankets made of coarse agave fibre, named *ichtilmates*, and some loads of agave leaves, named *metlontli*.

Their principal idol was Huitzilopochtli which for greater veneration was placed on the hill of Chapultepec in the City of Mexico. Aside from this there were other minor idols in the town of San Juan which was the temple and oracle to which the inhabitants of all neighboring towns flocked.

In the said town there was a very high pyramid temple which had [stairs with] three landing places [terraces] by means of which one ascended to the

summit. On its summit was a stone idol they named Tonacatecuhlli, made of a very hard, rough stone all of one piece. It was eighteen feet long, six feet wide and six feet thick, and faced the West.

In the level space in front of said temple, there was another small one, eighteen feet high, on which was an idol smaller than the first, named Micttlantecuhtli, which means Lord of the Underworld. This faced the first and was seated on a large stone six feet square. A little farther to the North was another [pyramid] temple slightly smaller than the first, which was called "the Hill of the Moon," on the top of which was another great idol nearly eighteen feet high which they named the Moon. Surrounding this [pyramid] temple were many others, in the largest of which were six other idols called "the Brethren of the Moon," to all of which the priests of Montezuma, the lord of Mexico, with the said Montezuma came to offer sacrifices, every twenty days. . . .

Every four-year period closed with a feast on the number twenty but in the bissextile year there were five days in excess and they then held a feast in a large square that was situated between the two pyramids. In the centre of this square there was a small platform about twelve feet high on which they punished evil-doers and delinquents.

DON FRANCISCO DE CASTANEDA
Official Report to Philip II, 1580

Alexander von Humboldt set sail for America on June 15, 1799. He took with him more than forty scientific instruments, and the five years he spent in Latin America were given to testing, measuring, and collecting data. Humboldt was an empiricist, an heir of the French Encyclopedists. He believed that natural laws govern natural phenomena, and that all phenomena of nature are linked together. His observations on Teotihuacán reflect his interest in the question of Asian origins of pre-Columbian civilizations.

The only ancient monuments in the Mexican valley which from their size or their masses can strike the eyes of an European are the remains of the two pyramids of San Juan de Teotihuacan, situated to the north-east of the lake of Tezcuco, consecrated to the sun and moon, which the Indians called Tonatiuh Ytzaqual, house of the sun, and Metzli Ytzaqual, house of the moon. According to the measurements made in 1803 by a young Mexican savant, Doctor Oteyza, the first pyramid, which is the most southern, has in its present state a base of . . . 645 feet in length, and . . . 171 feet of perpendicular elevation. The second, the pyramid of the moon, is . . . 30 feet lower, and its base is much less. These monuments, according to the accounts of the first travellers, and from the form which they yet exhibit, were the models of the Aztec teocallis. The nations whom the Spaniards found settled in New Spain attributed the pyramids of Teotihuacan to the Toultec nation; consequently their construction goes as far back as the eighth or ninth century; for the kingdom of Tolula lasted from 667 to 1031. The faces of these edifices are to within 52′ exactly placed from north to south, and from east to west. Their interior is clay, mixed with small stones. This kernel is covered with a thick wall of porous amygdaloid. We perceive, besides, traces of a bed of lime which covers the stones (the tetzontli) on the outside. Several authors of the sixteenth century pretend, according to an Indian tradition, that the interior of these pyramids is hollow. Boturini says that Siguenza, the Mexican geometrician, in vain endeavoured to pierce these edifices by a gallery. They formed four layers, of which three are only now perceivable, the injuries of time and the vegetation of the cactus and agaves having exercised their destructive influence on the exterior of these monuments. A stair of large hewn stones formerly led to their tops, where, according to the accounts of the first travellers, were statues covered with very thin lamina of gold. Each of the four principal layers was subdivided into small gradations of [3 feet 3 inches], in height, of which the edges are still distinguishable, which were covered with fragments of obsidian, that were undoubtedly the edge instruments with which the Toultec and Aztec priests in their barbarous sacrifices (*Papahua Tlemacazque or Teopixqui*) opened the chest of the human victims. . . .

It would be undoubtedly desirable to have the question resolved, whether these curious edifices, of which the one (*the Tonatiuh Ytzaqual*), according to the accurate measurement of my friend M. Oteyza, has a mass of [33,743,201 cubic feet], were entirely constructed by the hand of man, or whether the Toultecs took advantage of some natural hill which they covered over with stone and lime. This very question has been recently agitated with respect to several pyramids of Giza and Sacara; and it has become doubly interesting from the fantastical hypotheses which M. Witte has thrown out as to the origin of the monuments of colossal form in Egypt, Persepolis, and Palmyra. As neither the pyramids of Teotihuacan, nor that of Cholula, of which we shall afterwards have occasion to speak, have been diametrically pierced, it is impossible to speak with certainty of their interior structure. The Indian traditions, from which they are believed to be hollow, are vague and contradictory. Their situation in plains where no other hill is to be found renders it extremely probable that no natural rock serves for a kernel to these monuments. What is also very remarkable (especially if we call to mind the assertions of Pococke, as to the symmetrical position of the lesser pyramids of Egypt) is, that around the houses of the sun and moon of Teotihuacan we find a groupe, I may say a system, of pyramids, of scarcely [29 or 32 feet] of elevation. These monuments, of which there are several hundreds, are disposed in very large streets which follow exactly the direction of the parallels, and of the meridians, and which terminate in the four faces of the two great pyramids. The lesser pyramids are more frequent towards the southern side of the temple of the moon than towards the temple of the sun: and, according to the tradition of the country, they were dedicated to the stars. It appears certain enough that they served as burying places for the chiefs of tribes. All the plain which the Spaniards, from a word of the language of the island of Cuba, call *Llano de los Cues*, bore formerly in the Aztec and Toultec languages the name of *Micaotl*, or road of the dead. What analogies with the monuments of the old continent! And this Toultec people, who, on arriving in the seventh century on the Mexican soil, constructed on a uniform plan several of those colossal monuments, those truncated pyramids divided by layers, like the temple of Belus at Babylon, whence did they take the model of these edifices? Were they of Mongol race? Did they descend from a common stock with the Chinese, the Hiong-nu, and the Japanese?

ALEXANDER VON HUMBOLDT
Political Essay on the Kingdom of New Spain, 1811

The man who first awakened widespread interest in the ruins of Central America was the New York lawyer and world traveler John L. Stephens. Stephens had written a best-seller on Arabia and the Holy Land prior to setting out in search of the ancient stone cities of Mexico, Honduras and Guatemala in 1839. His first destination was the ruins of Copán.

The wall was of cut stone, well laid, and in a good state of preservation. We ascended by large stone steps, in some places perfect, and in others thrown down by trees which had grown up between the crevices, and reached a terrace, the form of which it was impossible to make out, from the density of the forest in which it was enveloped. Our guide cleared a way with his machete, and we passed, as it lay half buried in the earth, a large fragment of stone elaborately sculptured, and came to the angle of a structure with steps on the sides, in form and appearance, so far as the trees would enable us to make it out, like the sides of a pyramid. Diverging from the base, and working our way through the thick woods, we came upon a square stone column, about fourteen feet high and three feet on each side, sculptured in very bold relief, and on all four of the sides, from the base to the top. The front was the figure of a man curiously and richly dressed, and the face, evidently a portrait, solemn, stern, and well fitted to excite terror. The back was of a different design, unlike anything we had ever seen before, and the sides were covered with hieroglyphics. This our guide called an "Idol;" and before it, at a distance of three feet, was a large block of stone, also sculptured with figures and emblematical devices, which he called an altar. The sight of this unexpected monument put at rest at once and forever, in our minds, all uncertainty in regard to the character of American antiquities, and gave us the assurance that the objects we were in search of were interesting, not only as the remains of an unknown people, but as works of art, proving, like newly-discovered historical records, that the people who once occupied the Continent of America were not savages. With an interest perhaps stronger than we had ever felt in wandering among the ruins of Egypt, we followed our guide, who, sometimes missing his way, with a constant and vigorous use of his machete, conducted us through the thick forest among half-buried fragments, to fourteen monuments of the same character and appearance, some with more elegant designs, and some in workmanship equal to the finest monuments of the Egyptians; one displaced from its pedestal by enormous roots; another locked in the close embrace of branches of trees, and almost lifted out of the earth; another hurled to the ground, and bound down by huge vines and creepers; and one standing, with its altar before it, in a grove of trees which grew around it, seemingly to shade and shroud it as a sacred thing; in the solemn stillness of the woods, it seemed a divinity mourning over a fallen people. The only sounds that disturbed the quiet of this buried city were the noise of monkeys moving among the tops of the trees, and the cracking of dry branches broken by their weight. . . .

We returned to the base of the pyramidal structure, and ascended by regular stone steps, in some places forced apart by bushes and saplings, and in others thrown down by the growth of large trees, while some remained entire. In parts they were ornamented with sculptured figures and rows of death's heads. Climbing over the ruined top, we reached a terrace overgrown with trees, and, crossing it, descended by stone steps into an area so covered with trees that at first we could not make out its form, but which, on clearing the way with the machete, we ascertained to be a square, and with steps on all sides almost as perfect as those of the Roman amphitheatre. The steps were ornamented with sculpture, and on the south side, about half way up, forced out of its place by roots, was a colossal head, evidently a portrait. We ascended these steps, and reached a broad terrace a hundred feet high, overlooking the river, and supported by the wall which we had seen from the opposite bank. The whole terrace was covered with trees, and even at this height from the ground were two gigantic Ceibas, or wild cotton trees of India, above twenty feet in circumference, extending their half-naked roots fifty or a hundred feet around, binding down the ruins, and shading them with their wide-spreading branches. We sat down on the very edge of the wall and strove in vain to penetrate the mystery by which we were surrounded. Who were the people that built this city? In the ruined cities of Egypt, even in the long-lost Petra, the stranger knows the story of the people whose vestiges are around him. America, say historians, was peopled by savages; but savages never reared these structures, savages never carved these stones. We asked the Indians who made them, and their dull answer was "Quien sabe?" "who knows?"

There were no associations connected with the place; none of those stirring recollections which hallow Rome, Athens, and "The world's great mistress on the Egyptian plain;" but architecture, sculpture, and painting, all the arts which embellish life, had flourished in this overgrown forest; orators, warriors, and statesmen, beauty, ambition, and glory, had lived and passed away, and none knew that such things had been, or could tell of their past experience. Books, the records of knowledge, are silent on this theme. The city was desolate. No remnant of this race hangs round the ruins, with traditions handed down from father to son, and from generation to generation. It lay before us like a shattered bark in the midst of the ocean, her masts gone, her name effaced, her crew perished, and none to tell whence she came, to whom she belonged, how long on her voyage, or what caused her destruction; her lost people to be traced only by some fancied resemblance in the construction of the vessel, and, perhaps, never to be known at all. The place where we sat, was it a citadel from which an unknown people had sounded the trumpet of war? or a temple for the worship of the God of peace? or did the inhabitants worship the idols made with their own hands, and offer sacrifices on the stones before them? All was mystery, dark impenetrable mystery, and every circumstance increased it.

It is unfortunate that in awakening interest in pre-Columbian sites, Stephens set the stage for their plunder. He was guilty of piracy himself. Sadly, his justification for such actions — that such works are unappreciated in their country of origin — still has proponents today.

The general character of these ruins is the same as at Copan. The monuments are much larger, but they are sculptured in lower relief, less rich in design, and more faded and worn, probably being of a much older date.

Of one thing there is no doubt: a large city once stood there; its name is lost, its history unknown. . . . For centuries it has lain as completely buried as if covered with the lava of Vesuvius. Every traveller from Yzabal to Guatimala has passed within three hours of it; we ourselves had done the same; and yet there it lay, . . . unvisited, unsought, and utterly unknown.

The morning after Mr. C. returned I called upon Señor Payes, the only one of the brothers then in Guatimala, and opened a negotiation for the purchase of these ruins. Besides their entire newness and immense interest as an unexplored field of antiquarian research, the monuments were but a mile from the river, the ground was level to the bank, and the river from that place was navigable; the city might be transported bodily and set up in New-York. I expressly stated (and my reason for doing so will be obvious) that I was acting in this matter on my own account, that it was entirely a personal affair; but Señor Payes would consider me as acting for my government, and said, what I am sure he meant, that if his family was as it had been once, they would be proud to present the whole to the United States; in that country they were not appreciated, and he would be happy to contribute to the cause of science in ours; but they were impoverished by the convulsions of the country; and, at all events, he could give me no answer till his brothers returned, who were expected in two or three days. Unfortunately, as I believe for both of us, Señor Payes consulted with the French consul general, who put an exaggerated value upon the ruins, referring him to the expenditure of several hundred thousand dollars by the French government in transporting one of the obelisks of Luxor from Thebes to Paris. Probably, before the speculating scheme referred to, the owners would have been glad to sell the whole tract, consisting of more than fifty thousand acres, with everything on it, known and unknown, for a few thousand dollars. I was anxious to visit them myself, and learn with more certainty the possibility of their removal, but was afraid of increasing the extravagance of his notions. His brothers did not arrive, and one of them unfortunately died on the road. I had not the government for paymaster; it might be necessary to throw up the purchase on account of the cost of removal; and I left an offer with Mr. Savage, the result of which is still uncertain; but I trust that when these pages reach the hands of the reader, two of the largest monuments will be on their way to this city.

JOHN L. STEPHENS
Incidents of Travel in Central America, Chiapas, and Yucatán, 1841

PYRAMIDS TO THE SUN AND MOON

Frances Calderón de la Barca, the observant Scottish-born wife of a Spanish diplomat, was in Mexico from 1838 to 1843. The informal, intuitive letters she sent her family and friends were eventually shaped into a book, Life in Mexico. *Though the work suffers from several rather glaring misconceptions (for example, Tenochtitlán, not Teotihuacán, was destroyed by Cortés; the ruins never served as an "Aztec or Toltec Père-la-Chaise"), it was perceptive enough to be used as a guide by American officers in the Mexican war of 1846–48.*

The road grew more picturesque as we advanced, and at length our attention was arrested by the sight of the two great pyramids, which rise to the east of the town of San Juan Teotihuacan, which are mentioned by Humboldt, and have excited the curiosity and attention of every succeeding traveller. The huge masses were consecrated to the sun and moon, which, in the time of Cortes, were there represented by two vast stone idols, covered with gold. The conquerors made use of the gold, and broke the idols in pieces, by order of the first bishop of Mexico. Unfortunately, our time was too limited to give them more than a passing observation. Fragments of obsidian, in the form of knives and of arrows, with which the priests opened the breasts of their human victims, are still to be found there; and numerous small idols, made of baked clay, are to be seen both there and in the plains adjoining. The Indians rather dislike to guide travellers to these pyramids, and their reluctance to do so has increased the popular belief of the existence of great concealed treasures near or in them.

The whole plain on which these great pyramids stand was formerly called Micoatl, or the Pathway of the Dead; and the hundreds of smaller pyramids which surround the larger ones (the Temples of the Sun and Moon) are symmetrically disposed in wide streets, forming a great burial-plain, composed perhaps of the dust of their ancient warriors, an Aztec or Toltec Père-la-Chaise, or rather a roofless Westminster Abbey. So few of the ancient *teocallis* now remain, and these being nearly the only traces now existing of that extraordinary race, we regretted the more not being able to devote some time to their examination. Fanaticism and policy induced the Spanish conquerors to destroy these heathen temples; and when we recollect that at the time of the Reformation in civilized England, the most splendid Catholic edifices were made level with the ground, . . . we can have little wonder or blame to bestow upon Cortes, who, in the excitement of the siege, gave orders for the destruction of these blood-stained sanctuaries.

MME. CALDERON DE LA BARCA
Life in Mexico, 1838

The American historian William H. Prescott completed his exhaustively researched History of the Conquest of Mexico *in 1843. Prescott described in detail the daily life, manners, and mores of the ancient Aztecs. Never having visited the ruins himself, he relied in part on his correspondence with Frances Calderón de la Barca for his very visual description of Teotihuacán.*

The monuments of San Juan Teotihuacan are, with the exception of the temple of Cholula, the most ancient remains, probably, on the Mexican soil. They were found by the Aztecs, according to their traditions, on their entrance into the country, when Teotihuacan, *the habitation of the gods,* now a paltry village, was a flourishing city, the rival of Tula, the great Toltec capital. The two principal pyramids were dedicated to *Tonatiuh,* the Sun, and *Meztli,* the Moon. The former, which is considerably the larger, is found by recent measurements to be six hundred and eighty-two feet long at the base, and one hundred and eighty feet high, dimensions not inferior to those of some of the kindred monuments of Egypt. They were divided into four stories, of which three are now discernible, while the vestiges of the intermediate gradations are nearly effaced. In fact, time has dealt so roughly with them, and the materials have been so much displaced by the treacherous vegetation of the tropics, muffling up with its flowery mantle the ruin which it causes, that it is not easy to discern, at once, the pyramidal form of the structures. The huge masses bear such resemblance to the North American mounds, that some have fancied them to be only natural eminences shaped by the hand of man into a regular form, and ornamented with the temples and terraces, the wreck of which still covers their slopes. But others, seeing no example of a similar elevation in the wide plain in which they stand, infer . . . that they are wholly of an artificial construction.

The interior is composed of clay mixed with pebbles, incrusted on the surface with the light porous stone *tetzontli,* so abundant in the neighboring quarries. Over this was a thick coating of stucco, resembling, in its reddish color, that found in the ruins of Palenque. According to tradition, the pyramids are hollow, but hitherto the attempt to discover the cavity in that dedicated to the Sun has been unsuccessful. In the smaller mound, an aperture has been found on the southern side, at two thirds of the elevation. It is formed by a narrow gallery, which, after penetrating to the distance of several yards, terminates in two pits or wells. The largest of these is about fifteen feet deep; and the sides are faced with unbaked bricks; but to what purpose it was devoted, nothing is left to show. It may have been to hold the ashes of some powerful chief, like the solitary apartment discovered in the great Egyptian pyramid. That these monuments were dedicated to religious uses, there is no doubt; and it would be only conformable to the practice of Antiquity in the eastern continent, that they should have served for tombs, as well as temples.

Distinct traces of the latter destination are said to be visible on the summit of the smaller pyramid, consisting of the remains of stone walls showing a building of considerable size and strength. There are no remains on the top of the pyramid of the Sun. But the traveller, who will take the trouble to ascend its bald summit, will be amply compensated by the glorious view it will open to him; — towards the south-east, the hills of Tlascala, surrounded by their green plantations and cultivated corn-fields, in the midst of which stands the little village, once the proud capital of the republic. Somewhat further to the south, the eye passes across the beautiful plains lying around the city of Puebla de los Angeles, founded by the old Spaniards, and still rivalling, in the splendor of its churches, the most brilliant capitals of Europe; and far in the west he may behold the Valley of Mexico, spread out like a map, with its diminished lakes, its princely capital rising in still greater glory from its ruins, and its rugged hills gathering darkly around it, as in the days of Montezuma.

The summit of this larger mound is said to have been crowned by a temple, in which was a colossal statue of its presiding deity, the Sun, made of one entire block of stone, and facing the east. Its breast was protected by a plate of burnished gold and silver, on which the first rays of the rising luminary rested. An antiquary, in the early part of the last century, speaks of having seen some fragments of the statue. It was still standing, according to report, on the invasion of the Spaniards, and was demolished by the indefatigable Bishop Zumarraga, whose hand fell more heavily than that of Time itself on the Aztec monuments.

Around the principal pyramids are a great number of smaller ones, rarely exceeding thirty feet in height, which, according to tradition, were dedicated to the stars, and served as sepulchres for the great men of the nation. They are arranged symmetrically in avenues terminating at the sides of the great pyramids, which face the cardinal points. The plain on which they stand was called *Micoatl,* or "Path of the Dead." The laborer, as he turns up the ground, still finds there numerous arrowheads, and blades of obsidian, attesting the warlike character of its primitive population.

What thoughts must crowd on the mind of the traveller, as he wanders amidst these memorials of the past; as he treads over the ashes of the generations who reared these colossal fabrics, which take us from the present into the very depths of time! But who were their builders? Was it the shadowy Olmecs, whose history, like that of the ancient Titans, is lost in the mists of fable? or, as commonly reported, the peaceful and industrious Toltecs, of whom all that we can glean rests on traditions hardly more secure? What has become of the races who built them? Did they remain on the soil, and mingle and become incorporated with the fierce Aztecs who succeeded them? Or did they pass on to the South, and find a wider field for the expansion of their civilization, as shown by the higher character of the architectural remains in the distant regions of Central America and Yucatan? It is all a mystery — over which Time has thrown an impenetrable veil, that no mortal hand may raise. A nation has passed away, — powerful, populous, and well advanced in refinement, as attested by their monuments, — but it has perished without a name. It has died and made no sign!

WILLIAM H. PRESCOTT
History of the Conquest of Mexico, 1843

In his search for the Toltecs, the French archaeologist Désiré Charnay excavated many hitherto unknown ancient sites in Mexico. Charnay was correct in theorizing that Tula was the ancient capital of the Toltecs. His pioneer excavations there and at Teotihuacán have been of inestimable value, even though his theory that the Toltecs also settled Teotihuacán has never been satisfactorily proven.

We returned to the ruins, where I look forward to bringing to light a house, that I may prove Teotihuacán to have been as much a Toltec city as Tula. Whilst casting about where to begin I noticed parts of walls, broken cement and terraces, north of the river, when forthwith we cleared away the rubbish until we reached the floor, following the walls, corners, and openings of the various apartments, as we had done at Tula; and when three days later the engineer, Mr. P. Castro, joined us, ten rooms, forming part of the house, had been unearthed. He was so surprised at our success that, stopping short, he exclaimed: "Why, it is our Tula palace over again!"

And so it was — inner courts, apartments on different levels, everything as we had found before, save that here the rooms were much larger and most supported by pillars; one of these chambers measures 49 feet on one side, that is 732 feet in circumference. The walls, nearly six feet seven inches thick, are built of stone and mortar, incrusted with deep cement, sloping up about three feet and terminating perpendicularly. The centre of the room is occupied by six pillars, on which rose stone, brick, or wood columns bearing the roof.

This is undoubtedly a palace, and these are the reception rooms; the sleeping apartments were behind; unfortunately they lie under cultivated ground covered with Indian corn, so we are not permitted to disturb them. In the large room we observed small stone rings fixed to the wall, and on each side of the entrance, also fixed to the wall, two small painted slabs. What had been their use? To support lights at night? . . .

Here also the floors and walls are coated with mortar, stucco, or cement, save that in the dwellings of the rich, necessarily few, they are ornamented with figures, as principal subject, with a border like an Aubusson carpet. The colours are not all effaced, red, black, blue, yellow, and white, are still discernible; a few examples of these frescoes are to be seen in the Trocadéro.

I am convinced that numerous treasures might be brought to light were regular excavations to be made, but the Mexican Government, which would have most interest in such a work, does not seem to care to undertake it.

Leaving my men under the direction of Colonel Castro, I return to the "Path of Death," composed of a great number of small mounds, *Tlateles,* the tombs of great men. They are arranged symmetrically in avenues terminating at the sides of the great pyramids, on a plain of some 620 feet to 975 feet in length; fronting them are cemented steps, which must have been used as seats by the spectators during funeral ceremonies or public festivities. On the left, amidst a mass of ruins, are broken pillars, said to have belonged to a temple; the huge capitals have some traces of sculpture. Next comes a quadrangular block, of which a cast is to be found in the main gallery of the Trocadéro.

In the course of my excavations I had found now and again numerous pieces of worked obsidian, precious stones, beads, etc., within the circuit of ants' nests, which these busy insects had extracted from the ground in digging their galleries; and now on the summit of the lesser pyramid I again came upon my friends and among the things I picked out of their nests was a perfect earring of obsidian, very small and as thin as a sheet of paper. It is not so curious at it seems at first, for we are disturbing a ground formed by fifty generations.

Glass does not seem to have been known to the Indians, for although Tezcatlipoca was often figured with a pair of spectacles, they may only have been figurative ones like those of the manuscripts, terra-cotta, or bassi-rilievi, for there is nothing to show that they had any idea of optics.

I now went back to my men, when to my great delight I found they had unearthed two large slabs showing the entrance of two sepulchres; they were the first I had yet found, and considering them very important, I immediately telegraphed to Messrs. Chavero and Berra, both of whom are particularly interested in American archaeology. . . .

One of the slabs closed a vault, and the other a cave with perpendicular walls; we went down the former by a flight of steps in fairly good condition, yet it was a long and rather dangerous affair, for we were first obliged to demolish a wall facing us, in which we found a skull, before we could get to the room which contained the tombs. The vases within them are exactly like those we found in the plaza, except that one is filled with a fatty substance — like burnt flesh — mixed with some kind of stuff, the woof of which is still discernible, besides beads of serpentine, bones of dogs and squirrels, knives of obsidian twisted by the action of fire. We know from Sahagun that the dead were buried with their clothes and their dogs to guide and defend them in their long journey: "When the dead were ushered into the presence of the king of the nether world, *Mictlantecutli,* they offered him papers, bundles of sticks, pine-wood and perfumed reeds, together with loosely twisted threads of white and red cotton, a manta, a maxtli, tunics, and shirts. When a woman died her whole wardrobe was carefully put aside, and a portion burnt eighty days after; this operation was repeated on that day twelve months for four years, when everything that had belonged to the deceased was finally consumed. The dead then came out of the first circle to go successively through nine others encompassed by a large river. On its banks were a number of dogs which helped their owners to cross the river; whenever a ghost neared the bank, his dog immediately jumped into the river and swam by his side or carried him to the opposite bank." It was on this account that Indians had always several small dogs about them. . . .

But to return to our tombstones. They are both alike, being about five feet high, three feet five inches broad, and six inches and a half thick. The upper side is smooth, the lower has some carving in the shape of a cross, four big tears or drops of water, and a pointed tongue in the centre, which, starting from the bottom of the slab, runs up in a line parallel to the drops.

Knowing how general was the worship of Tlaloc among the Indians, I conjectured this had been a monument to the god of rain, to render him propitious to the dead; a view shared and enlarged upon by Dr. Hamy in a paper read before the Academie des Sciences in November, 1882; and that I should be in accord with the eminent specialist on American antiquities is a circumstance to make me proud. I may add that the carving of this slab is similar to that of the cross on the famous basso-rilievo at Palenque; so that the probability of the two monuments having been erected to the god of rain is much strengthened thereby.

As our slabs are far more archaic than those at Palenque, we think we are justified in calling them earlier in time — the parent samples of the later ones. Nor is our assumption unsupported, for we shall subsequently find that the cult of Tlaloc and Quetzalcoatl was carried by the Toltecs in their distant peregrinations. These slabs, therefore, and the pillars we found in the village, acquire a paramount importance in establishing the affiliation of Toltec settlements in Tabasco, Yucatan, and other places, furnishing us with further data in regard to certain monuments at Palenque, the steles of Tikal, and the massive monolith idols of Copan.

I next attacked the terraced court fronting the palace towards the Path of Death, and the amount of constructions and substructures we came upon is almost beyond belief: inclined stuccoed walls crossing each other in all directions, flights of steps leading to terraces within the pyramid, ornaments, pottery, and detritus; so much so that the pyramid might not improperly be called a necropolis, in which the living had their dwellings.

In a word, our campaign at Teotihuacan was as successful as our campaign at Tula. We were attended by the same good fortune, and the reader whom such things may interest will find a bas-relief of both Toltec palaces, and of one of the tombstones, in the Trocadéro.

DÉSIRÉ CHARNAY
The Ancient Cities of the New World, 1884

Graham Greene visited Mexico in the spring of 1938. The author of The Power and the Glory *found Teotihuacán cold and impersonal, "as inhuman as a problem in algebra."*

In the great grey courtyard of Teotihuacán, surrounded by the platforms of small pyramidal temples, you do get the sense of a continent over the world's edge — a flatness, a vacancy, through which peer plumed serpents and faces like gas-masks over orifices that might be the mouths of Lewis guns or flame-throwers. Archaeologists maintain theories of what happened here from the number of steps in each pyramid — mathematical computations that lead to a human sacrifice or a struggle between rival cults, rather in the same way as the British Israelites foretell the future from the comparative measurements of the Egyptian pyramids. It is fantastic — and credible. The mathematical sense seems to have run riot — everything is symmetrical; it is important that the Pyramid of the Sun should be sixty-six metres high and have five terraces and the Pyramid of the Moon be forty-four metres high and have — I forget how many terraces. Heresy here was not an aberration of human feeling — like the Manichaean — but a mathematical error. Death was important only as solving an equation. In the museum you see the little black glassy knives with which the breast of the sacrifice was opened — they look as hygienic as surgeons' instruments. Only the Temple of Quetzalcoatl is decorated — with horrors, serpents, and gas-masks — and he was the white Toltec god of culture, the mildest god of the lot, and was defeated by this stony mathematical discipline. One expects to see Q.E.D. written on the paving of the great court — the pyramids adding up correctly, the number of terraces multiplied by the number of steps, and divided by the square metres of the surface area, proving — something, something as inhuman as a problem in algebra.

GRAHAM GREENE
Another Mexico, 1939

MEXICO PAST AND PRESENT

Octavio Paz, Mexico's most distinguished living poet, is best known in English for a study of his country entitled The Labyrinth of Solitude. *Paz's powerful "Hymn Among Ruins" portrays a Mexico very much caught up in its pre-Columbian past.*

Crowned with itself, day stretches out its plumes.
A high and yellow cry,
a fountain of heat at the center of a sky
just and beneficent!
The seemings are lovely in this their moment of truth.
The sea mounting the coast
holds fast between the rocks, a dazzling spider;
the livid wound on the mountain glitters;
a few goats are a flock of stones,
the sun lays its golden egg, spilling over the sea.
All is god.
A broken statue,
pillars bitten by light,
ruins alive in a world of death in life!

Night falls over Teotihuacan.
High on the pyramid the boys smoke marijuana,
music of harsh guitars.
What grass, what water of life can give us life,
where will the word see light again,
the proportion that governs hymn and speech,
the dance, the city and the balances?
Mexican song exploding in a curse,
a star of colors that goes dark,
a stone sealing the gateway of our contact.
The earth tastes of worn-out earth.

Eyes see, hands touch.
A few things are enough:
prickly pear, the coral and thorny planet,
the hooded figs,
grapes tasting of resurrection
and clams, stubborn virginities,
salt, cheese, wine, bread of the sun.
From her high darkness an island girl looks at me,
a slim cathedral clothed in light.
Towers of salt, seen by the shore's green pines,
the white sails of the boats rise up.
Light builds its temples on the sea.

New York, London, Moscow.
Shadow creeps on the plain in phantom ivy,
swaying and shivering racemes,
its sparse down, its ratswarm.
Sometimes the weak sun shivers.
Reclining on hills that once were cities, Polyphemus yawns.
Down there, among the pits, a flock of men, dragging along.
(Domesticated, two-legged, their flesh
— recent religious penalties notwithstanding —
a delicacy for the wealthy class.
Only yesterday the common people considered them unclean.)

To see, to feel the lovely daily forms.
Buzzing of light, arrows, and wings.
It smells of blood, this winestain on the table.
Like the branches of coral stretched out in the water
I stretch my senses in the living hour:
the moment is complete, a yellow harmony.
Noon, rod of wheat heavy with minutes,
drink of eternity.

My thoughts are split, wind, entwine,
start again
and finally stand immobile, endless rivers,
delta of blood beneath a sun without twilight.
Must it all end in this splash of dead water?

Day, round day,
luminous orange with twenty-four sections,
all saturated with one single yellow sweetness!
Intelligence finally takes flesh in form
and the two enemy halves are reconciled —
now the conscience-mirror liquefies
and is a spring again, a fountain of legends:
Man, tree of images,
words that are flowers that are fruit that are the deeds.

OCTAVIO PAZ
"Hymn Among Ruins," 1948

REFERENCE

Chronology of Mesoamerican History

20,000 B.C.	Early man arrives in New World
c. 19,000	Earliest evidence of man in Mesoamerica
c. 7000–8000	Mammoth butchered at Santa Isabel Iztapan; Tepexpan man
c. 7000	Beginning of the Archaic period
c. 5000	Earliest evidence of domesticated maize
c. 2000	Earliest known pottery in Mesoamerica
c. 2000–1500	Beginning of the Formative or Preclassic period
c. 1500	Earliest farming villages in the Valley of Oaxaca
c. 1200	Beginning of the Olmec civilization
c. 1200–900	Olmecs settle at San Lorenzo, Veracruz
c. 1200–300	Small farming villages spring up in the Valley of Mexico; settlement of Tlapacoya, Tlatilco, Zacatenco, El Arbolillo, Ticomán
c. 1000–400	Olmecs settle at La Venta, Veracruz
c. 900–0	Olmecs settle at Tres Zapotes, Veracruz
c. 600	Zapotecs settle at Monte Albán in Oaxaca, date of earliest settlement in Teotihuacán Valley
c. 300–200	Round pyramid built at Cuilcuilco
c. 100	Beginning of the city of Teotihuacán
31	Oldest dated monument in the New World, Stela C at Tres Zapotes, carved
c. 1–150 A.D.	Great building activity at Teotihuacán; construction of the Pyramid of the Sun and Avenue of the Dead
c. 250	Maya develop the corbeled arch
c. 250–450	Great compound is built at Teotihuacán
292	Oldest dated Maya stela, Stela 29 at Tikal, Guatemala, carved
c. 300	Beginning of the Classic period; completion of the Pyramid of the Moon; Zapotecs commence rebuilding of Monte Albán
c. 400	Beginning of Teotihuacán influence at Monte Albán; Teotihuacán influence extends to Kaminaljuyú in highland Guatemala; beginnings of the Oaxacan, Gulf Coast, and Maya influences at Teotihuacán
c. 500	Teotihuacán reaches its peak
c. 600–1200	Rise and fall of city of El Tajín in Veracruz
c. 650–750	Decline and fall of Teotihuacán
692	Date carved on Temple of the Inscriptions at Maya city of Palenque
c. 700	Burning of the city of Teotihuacán; Mixtec records begin
c. 800	Murals painted at Bonampak
c. 800–1000	Xochicalco and Cholula dominate highland Mexico
889	Last stela with Long Count date erected in Maya lowlands
800–900	Classic Maya ceremonial centers abandoned
c. 900	Beginning of Postclassic period; metallurgy enters Mesoamerica; Mixtec peoples begin moving into the Valley of Oaxaca
909	Last Long Count date carved at La Muñeca in Quintana Roo
c. 935 or 947	Historical king Quetzalcoatl is born
c. 980	Toltec peoples found Tula
c. 987	Quetzalcoatl flees Tula; Toltecs conquer Chichén Itzá in Yucatán
c. 1000	End of Zapotec occupation of Monte Albán and rise of Mixtecs in Oaxaca; El Castillo erected
c. 1000–1200	Toltecs dominate most of Mesoamerica
1030–63	Eight Deer unites most of the Mixtecs
c. 1168	Toltecs abandon Tula; Aztecs enter Valley of Mexico
c. 1344–45	Aztecs found Tenochtitlán and Tlaltelolco
1428	Aztecs defeat the Tepanecs and begin their domination of Mexico
c. 1450	Fall of the Postclassic Maya capital of Mayapan
1502–20	Reign of Moctezuma II
1517	Spaniards under Cordoba first encounter the Maya of Yucatán
1519	Arrival of Cortés; capture of Moctezuma
1520	Moctezuma killed; Cuithalhuac reigns briefly; Cortés and his party are first Europeans to view Teotihuacán
1521	Cuauhtémoc becomes the last Aztec ruler; Tenochtitlán falls to the Spaniards
1524	Death of Cuauhtémoc
1697	Fall of Tayasal, the last Maya kingdom
1810	Beginning of the Mexican War of Independence
1839	Stephens and Catherwood explore Central America, uncovering ancient Maya sites
1846–48	War between Mexico and the United States
1864	First survey of Teotihuacán made
1876	Porfirio Diáz becomes provisional president, beginning era of personal dictatorship
1905–10	Batres "restores" Pyramid of the Sun
1910	Mexican Revolution begins
1924	Gamio drives tunnel through Pyramid of the Sun
1928	George Vaillant begins excavations of Preclassic sites in the Valley of Mexico
1932	Alfonso Caso finds richest treasure in Mesoamerica in Tomb No. 7 at Monte Albán
1939	Matthew Stirling unearths Stela C at Tres Zapotes, first Olmec site to be excavated
1941–43	Stirling excavates La Venta, first major Olmec center to be uncovered
1949–52	Alberto Ruz discovers a rich tomb in pyramid at Palenque
1960	René Millon begins extensive mapping project at Teotihuacán
1962–64	Mexicans carry out major excavations and restorations at Teotihuacán
1964	National Museum of Anthropology opens in Chapultapec Park

Guide to Pre-Columbian Sites

A civilization, according to Arnold J. Toynbee, arises in response to a challenge. "Creation is the outcome of an encounter, . . . genesis is a product of interaction," states the noted British historian. In Mesoamerica, the challenge was an intractable terrain. To the south and along the Gulf Coast, the lush, verdant rainforest is all-enveloping, a formidable obstacle to human endeavor. Conversely, the Yucatán Peninsula is bleak and arid, treeless and almost barren. But these and other challenges were answered; civilizations arose, flourished and then, inexplicably in so many cases, fell.

Unfortunately, excepting the Maya and the Mixtec, we possess little in the way of recorded histories of these civilizations. They did, however, bequeath us the legacy of their art and their architecture, and it is from these sources that we are able to ascertain where and when civilizations developed and trace certain influences they seem to have had in common.

The ancient pyramid of **Cuicuilco** — grim and foreboding — is very much in keeping with the bleak volcanic landscape of which it is a part. Situated on the southern periphery of Mexico City, it was most certainly built by Preclassic peoples in approximately the fourth century B.C. Although not a true pyramid (its base is circular rather than square), it nevertheless contains all the elements of the truncated pyramid design found again and again in Mesoamerican architecture. Pyramids of this type — of which Cuicuilco remains the earliest example — always had a religious function, serving as a platform for an altar or temple.

The Cuicuilco pyramid consists of a series of superimposed truncated cones. Although it is approximately sixty feet high, more than one third of its height was covered by lava from a 100 B.C. eruption of the nearby Xitli Volcano. The pyramid's original diameter was 369 feet; four rows of steps lead to the platform on which a temple once stood.

Fifty-five miles north of Mexico City lies **Tula**, the ancient capital of the Tol-tecs. The Toltecs are thought to have arrived in the Valley of Mexico in about A.D. 900. While they absorbed much of their culture from nearby Teotihuacán, they were a decidedly more martial people.

The main temple-pyramid at Tula was almost certainly dedicated to Quetzalcoatl, the Feathered Serpent. Although the temple that once graced the crest of the five-stepped pyramid has disappeared, we are able to ascertain from the breadth of the temple platform that it was of immense proportions. To roof over such a large area, the Toltecs hit upon the idea of using free-standing supports. No trace of the roof remains, but numerous pillars and columns — some decorated with reliefs, others carved into colossal warriors — have survived.

The Atlantes, as the warrior columns are called, are each fifteen feet tall. Four have been reconstructed, though there were probably many more. Each of these wears a butterfly-shaped breastplate and carries a sling and spearthrower. Two other columns of note have been fashioned into plumed serpents whose gaping jaws rest on the ground; upright tails once provided support for the lintels of the temple's antechamber.

Adjoining the main pyramid is the *coatepantli*, or serpent wall. One hundred and thirty feet long and seven feet high, the wall is adorned with a frieze depicting snakes devouring skeletal-like human figures. Serpent walls of this type were a feature of Mexican architecture from the Toltec period onward.

The Toltecs are thought to have remained in Tula for about two hundred years. They left the area in 1168, probably under pressures exerted by the Chichimecs and other recently arrived nomadic tribes.

According to Indian legend, after Quetzalcoatl left Tula, he spent twenty years in **Cholula**. This legend, stripped of its metaphor, illustrates the migration of the Toltec people, who were driven eastward by the invading Chichimecs. Toltec architectural skill is clearly in evidence at Cholula, seventy-five miles east of Mexico City and site of the largest pyramid in Mexico.

Called the Great Pyramid, it is badly deteriorated. Indeed, it more resembles a natural hill than a man-made structure; a great mound covered with foliage with a quaint colonial church perched on its summit. However, excavations of the site have revealed that at one time the base of the pyramid covered an area of forty-two acres — almost four times that of the Pyramid of Cheops in Egypt.

Sometime between A.D. 750–900 (the period corresponding with the destruction of Teotihuacán and building of Tula), one of the oldest known fortresses in Mesoamerica was built. Not only does **Xochicalco** form an important cultural bridge between two epochs but, because of its central location twenty-four miles south of Cuernavaca, it also forms a bridge between northern and southern Mesoamerican cultures.

Xochicalco was built on a sugarloaf mountain 430 feet above a wide plain. The main temple, La Malinche, is 54½ feet high on a base that measures 69 feet by 61 feet. The most unusual part of the structure is the ornate frieze that surrounds the temple's base. Eight plumed serpents face towards the four corners of the monument. Between the coils of these great snakes are seated beautifully carved human figures wearing elaborate headdresses that are strikingly Mayan in design.

There is also a ball court at Xochicalco, a long rectangle flanked on either side by a platform. The playing surface slopes upward toward the outer edges of the court and the whole is strongly reminiscent of the Maya ball court at Copán.

The magnificent Aztec capital of **Tenochtitlán** was utterly destroyed by the Spaniards, and Mexico City was built on the rubble of the city in the lake. The only remains of Tenochtitlán that are visible today are some ruins situated on Guatemala Street in the center of the Mexican capital. Thought to be part of the huge pyramid dedicated jointly to the rain god Tlaloc and to Huitzilopochtli, the god of war, the ruins consist of several flights of steps, a marble pavement, and a snake's head carved in stone.

Through descriptions of the great pyramid that exist in the narratives of those who destroyed it, we can surmise that it probably looked very much like the pyramid of **Tenayuca**. A provincial religious monument just outside Tenochtitlán, the Tenayuca pyramid went through six phases of reconstruction, the last of which bears the imprint of the Aztec style.

The original structure is thought to have been built by the Chichimecs. It was a four-stepped pyramid twenty-five feet high on a base thirty-seven feet by ninety-six feet. As new outer layers were added, the pyramid grew tremendously. Today its base is 192 feet by 155 feet and it is 63 feet high. Its walls rise steeply in a series of terraces to a flat summit.

Like the great temple at Tenochtitlán, the stairway scaling the pyramid's western façade is divided in two by a central balustrade. It seems plausible that this double stairway led to two separate shrines on the pyramid's summit. No trace of these has been found, but dual use of a single pyramid seems to have been characteristic of Aztec architecture; it was certainly the case with the Tenochtitlán pyramid.

To the north and south of the monument are low platforms, each supporting a large coiled serpent. On three sides of the pyramid, 138 projecting blocks of stone have been rudely fashioned into open-jawed snakes. These sculptures have none of the fine carving and delicate detail found at Tula and Xochicalco. In comparison, they are quite crude.

In the middle of Veracruz, a civilization called the **Tajin** culture grew up. Although there are parallels with the culture of Teotihuacán and other features which suggest Olmec influences, these were a separate people about whom little is known. A completely individual architectural and art style developed at Tajin, the main characteristic of which is the niche.

The seven-stepped Niche Pyramid is sixty feet high and has a base that is one hundred and twenty feet square. Its temple is still discernible, but by far its most unusual features are the square niches that decorate the vertical walls of each level of the pyramid. The steeply rising stairway was added later, but it too is embellished with niches.

Monte Albán, the most important Zapotec religious site, lies atop high, treeless hills 1,200 feet above and six miles southwest of the city of Oaxaca. One of the oldest sites in Mexico, Monte Albán was occupied from as early as 1000 B.C. until the coming of the Spanish in 1522. Like Teotihuacán, it is divided into distinctly different periods.

Little is known about the people of the first and second periods of Monte Albán, but their art indicates a strong Olmec influence. These people were replaced or absorbed by the Zapotecs in the fourth century A.D., and the Zapotecs occupy the third and fourth periods. They in turn were superseded by the Mixtecs, who in the fourteenth century initiated the fifth and final period of Monte Albán.

The supreme achievement of Monte Albán — the grandeur of conception with which it was laid out — is decidely Zapotec. These people were superb architects, with a profound understanding of spatial relationships. Like Teotihuacán, Monte Albán was a city of the gods. Unlike Teotihuacán, it seems to have been largely uninhabited. Supplicants only visited the site, and the absence of dwelling places further adds to Monte Albán's sense of spaciousness.

Monte Albán is composed of numerous building complexes, but the axes of all the buildings run parallel to one another. In addition, the levels of the various building compounds interrelate; the structures in the center of the site are lower than those on the edges.

Another interesting architectural feature found at Monte Albán is unusually broad flights of steps. For example, the steps leading to the large main pyramid are forty-five yards wide; the widest in Mesoamerica. The stairs were counterbalanced by massive temple pillars six feet in diameter, but only the stumps of these have survived.

One of the most beautiful — and certainly one of the most mysterious — works of art at Monte Albán is the frieze that decorated a pyramid on the west of the site. Called the *Danzantes*, or "Dancers," it dates from 500–200 B.C. and is composed of more than 140 clearly defined male nudes. The faces of these figures all have the thick nose and deep slant of the mouth characteristic of Olmec sculpture. The subjects are shown in a variety of poses; walking, crawling, falling, standing, sitting, kneeling. But even when standing or sitting, they convey a strong sense of motion. Archaeologists are at a loss to explain the frieze's meaning. Were Indian artists perhaps illustrating the concept of the stream of life? Or are the figures merely supposed to represent captives or prisoners of war?

The Mixtecs who came after the Zapotecs made use of existing structures while at the same time leaving their own im-

UNITED STATES

GULF
OF
MEXICO

N

MEXICO

SIERRA MADRE ORIENTAL

SIERRA MADRE OCCIDENTAL

HIDALGO

■ Tajín

■ Tula

TOLTECS

Teotihuacán ■

AZTECS

Tenayuca ■

TLAXCALA

MEXICO

Tenochtitlán

Cuicuilco ■

(Mexico City)

Xochicalco ■

■ Cholula

MORELOS

PUEBLA

VERACRUZ

YUCATAN

Chichén Itzá ■

M A Y A

CAMPECHE

TABASCO

SIERRA MADRE DEL SUR

GUERRERO

MIXTECS

■ Monte Albán

■ Mitla

OAXACA

ZAPOTECS

■ Palenque

■ Tikal

CHIAPAS

BELIZE
(BRITISH
HONDURAS)

GUATEMALA

HONDURAS

M A Y A

■ Copán

EL SALVADOR

*PACIFIC
OCEAN*

0   50   100   150   200   250

Scale of Miles

print. Tomb No. 7 at Monte Albán, for example, was built by the Zapotecs but was used by the Mixtecs as a mausoleum for their highest dignitaries. The intricately worked gold and silver ornaments, the carvings, ceramics, and other treasures found there are distinctly Mixtec and are outstanding examples of the superior craftsmenship they developed.

The Mixtecs advanced into the Zapotec city of **Mitla** as well as Monte Albán. Twenty-four miles southeast of Oaxaca, the site was used as a necropolis by both peoples. Its most notable features are walls adorned with what looks like a profusion of mosaics. In fact, they are not mosaics at all, but rather, stone slabs that have been carefully fitted together in a sophisticated geometric design.

Mesoamerican civilization reached its zenith with the Maya. Maya suzerainty extended over three distinct geographical regions; a mountainous area in Guatemala and western El Salvador, the dry, flat plains of Yucatán, and the tropical rainforests stretching across the states of Tabasco and Chiapas. Recorded history in Mexico begins with the Maya civilization. They also devised an accurate 365-day calendar and used the zero in their mathematical calculations while Europe was still in the Dark Ages. Their art and architecture rival those of classic periods of civilizations throughout the world.

Foremost among Maya religious centers was the sacred city of **Palenque**. Situated in the foothills of the Sierras in the state of Chiapas, Palenque is surrounded by a dense tropical rainforest whose thick foliage provides a dramatic backdrop for the gleaming white temples. While temples found atop pyramids in the Mexican plateau were usually built of wood, the Maya built theirs of stone. One of the technological steps that enabled them to do this was their invention of the corbeled arch in the third century A.D.

At least twelve temples have been discovered at Palenque, in addition to a palace complex set upon a platform three hundred feet long and two hundred and forty feet wide. This main palace contains numerous chambers, corridors, inner galleries, courts, and a four-story observatory tower, and it dominates the site.

Palenque's Temple of the Inscriptions is noted for its unique design motifs and graceful figures. In 1952, one of the most spectacular crypts in North America was discovered deep in the base of the pyramid. The crypt contained a sarcophagus ten feet long and seven feet wide, the cover of which had been embellished with carvings of stylized animals and flowers, glyphs, and the portrait of a young Maya noble, possibly a king. The skeleton inside had been buried with numerous jade artifacts, including a superb jade mosaic mask.

The largest Maya city, **Tikal**, is situated almost 190 miles due north of Guatemala City. Approximately six square miles of Tikal have been mapped, and in this area alone over three thousand separate constructions have been found. These include temples, palaces, shrines, ceremonial platforms, plazas, residences, ball courts, causeways, and a sweathouse that was used for ritual purposes.

The immensity of Tikal's Great Plaza is awe-inspiring. The plaza consists of four superimposed floors — the earliest was laid in about 150 B.C., the most recent in about A.D. 700 — covering an area of about two and one-half acres. On the eastern periphery, the Temple of the Giant Jaguar faces west toward the Temple of the Masks. To the north, a 280-foot stairway leads to the North Acropolis. The Central Acropolis lies to the south.

The Temple of the Giant Jaguar (so named for the motif on one of its carved lintels) consists of nine successive stepped-back terraces surmounted by a three-room temple and an ornamental roofcomb. The three rather small temple rooms all have Maya corbeled arches. The ornamental roofcomb is badly eroded but the outline of a regal figure flanked by elaborate scrolls and suggestions of serpents can still be discerned in strong sunlight.

As with the Temple of the Inscriptions at Palenque, the Temple of the Giant Jaguar was found to contain a rich tomb. A vaulted chamber deep within the pyramid yielded up a skeleton that had been buried with jade, pearls, pottery, alabaster, and orange-red shells from the Pacific. Some 180 pieces of carved jade alone adorned the remains of the deceased. It is unknown whether the death of this individual motivated the building of the pyramid or whether he was just a sufficiently high-ranking person to warrant burial there. Other temples at Tikal were also used for elaborate burials just prior to the start of construction.

The Temple of the Masks is in many ways a smaller version of the Temple of the Giant Jaguar. Directly opposite the latter, it has a carved roofcomb and a three-room temple with corbeled arches.

Unlike the Temple of the Giant Jaguar, it has only three stepped-back terraces instead of nine.

Tikal contains six more immense pyramids similar to the ones described, in addition to numerous palaces and some of the most superb stelae and altars ever found at Maya sites.

The second largest — and most southern — of the great Maya cities was **Copán**. Overlooking the Copán River from an altitude of two thousand feet, Copán covers seventy-five acres in what is today Honduras.

Copán is composed of five main plazas and numerous other smaller ones. Tiers of stone seats surround the enormous main plaza, giving it an almost Roman appearance. The eastern courtyard likewise contains tiers of stone seats, in addition to the spectacular Jaguar Stairway. Rampant stone jaguars, their coats at one time inlaid with rounded pieces of obsidian, flank the staircase.

The Reviewing Stand, a flight of five steps fifty-five feet wide, abuts on the western court. Two serpent gods, each with grotesque features and entwined by snakes, stand guard at the base of the stairway. The enigmatic Hieroglyphic Stairway, thirty feet wide with sixty-three steps, also rises in the western court. The treads of this stairway are decorated with approximately 2,500 glyphs — but of these, only dates have been deciphered; the rest remains a mystery.

For reasons still unknown, the conclusion of the Classic era saw the demise of the major Maya ceremonial sites. **Chichén Itzá**, near the Yucatán tip, was one of the few Maya cities to flourish after A.D. 900. Its resurgence was due to

an invasion by the Itzá, a people whose identity is still a matter of conjecture. Their culture strongly resembles that of the Toltecs — there are uncanny similarities between Tula and Chichén Itzá, although the two are more than eight hundred miles apart — but whether they were a Toltec people or a Maya people who had adopted the Quetzalcoatl cult and Toltec culture is unknown.

As at Tula, the Feathered Serpent is a prominent motif at Chichén Itzá. There are numerous representations of the god on low-relief sculpture, on the balustrades flanking steep stairways, and most notably on the twin columns that bisect the entrance to the Temple of the Warriors.

The Itzá built their main pyramid (today called El Castillo because a conquistador once mounted his cannons at its summit) over an existing Maya structure. It is seventy-eight feet high, a nine-stepped pyramid on a one-hundred-and-eighty-foot base. The pyramid has four separate staircases, one on each side, and these each contain ninety-one steps. The Temple of Kukulcán (the Maya equivalent of Quetzalcoatl) at the pyramid's peak contains two more serpent columns.

It is in this extensive use of columns that one finds a strong architectural similarity between Chichén Itzá and Tula. While the Maya corbeled arch represented a significant advance, it had its limitations. The Maya were only able to build roofs over narrow corridors. The Toltecs solved this problem by the introduction of columns which supported a roof made of square stone slabs resting on wooden beams. They were thus able to build roofs over rooms as wide as they were long. This techno-

logical advance is exemplied at Chichén Itzá in the Temple of the Warriors.

In many ways reminiscent of the Toltec temple at Tula, the Temple of the Warriors is almost square in plan and at one time had a large antechamber in front of its stepped pyramid. Unfortunately, the wooden beams upon which the roof slabs rested deteriorated, thus leaving only the so-called "Thousand Columns" standing. Both the antechamber columns and the temple itself bear the same martial motifs found at Tula; carvings of armed spearmen, eagles, and marching jaguars abound.

The civilizations of the Olmecs, the Zapotecs, the Mixtecs, the Toltecs, the Aztecs, and the Maya are no more. But there is a lesson to be learned in surveying the silent ruins that remain and it is most eloquently expressed by Toynbee. The historian is speaking chiefly of the Maya, but his observations apply to all the vanished civilizations of Mesoamerica: "The transitoriness of human achievement and the vanity of human wishes are poignantly exposed by the return of the forest, engulfing first the fields and then the houses and finally the palaces and temples themselves. Yet that is not the most significant lesson to be learnt from the present state of Copan or Tikal or Palenque. The ruins speak still more eloquently of the intensity of the struggle with the physical environment which the creators of the Mayan Civilization must have waged in their day. In her very revenge, which reveals her in all her gruesome power, Tropical Nature testifies to the courage and vigour of the men who once, if only for a season, succeeded in putting her to flight and keeping her at bay."

Selected Bibliography

Bernal, Ignacio. *The Olmec World*. Berkeley: University of California Press, 1969.

Coe, Michael D. *Mexico*. New York: Praeger Publishers, 1962.

Charnay, Désiré. *The Ancient Cities of the New World*. New York: Harper and Brothers, 1883.

Covarrubias, Miguel. *Indian Art of Mexico and Central America*. New York: Alfred A. Knopf, Inc., 1957.

Díaz del Castillo, Bernal. *The Discovery and Conquest of Mexico*, translated by A. P. Maudslay. New York: Farrar, Straus and Cudahy, Inc. 1956.

Deuel, Leo. *Conquistadors Without Swords*. New York: St. Martin's Press, 1967.

Hardoy, Jorge E. *Pre-Columbian Cities*. New York: Walker & Co., 1973.

von Hagen, Victor W. *Maya Explorer*. Norman: University of Oklahoma Press, 1948.

Paz, Octavio. *The Labyrinth of Solitude*. London: Allen Lane, 1967.

Prescott, W. H. *History of the Conquest of Mexico*. Philadelphia: J. B. Lippincott & Co., 1863.

Soustelle, Jacques. *The Daily Life of the Aztecs*. London: Weidenfeld and Nicolson Ltd., 1961.

Stephens, John Lloyd. *Incidents of Travel in Central America, Chiapas and Yucatán*. New Brunswick, N.J.: Rutgers University Press, 1949.

————. *Incidents of Travel in Yucatán*. Norman: University of Oklahoma Press, 1962.

Acknowledgments and Picture Credits

The Editors wish to extend their thanks to Atheneum Publishers for permission to reprint in chapters I, IV and V passages from the author's The Pleasures of Archaeology, *copyright © 1969, 1970 by Karl E. Meyer and published by Atheneum. The Editors also make grateful acknowledgment for the use of excerpted material from the following works:*

A Study of History by Arnold J. Toynbee. Edited by D. C. Somervell. Copyright © 1946 by Oxford University Press, Inc. The excerpt appearing on page 167 is reproduced by permission of Oxford University Press.

America's First Civilization by Michael D. Coe Copyright © 1968 by American Heritage Publishing Company, Inc. The excerpt appearing on page 45 is reproduced by permisson of American Heritage Publishing Company, Inc.

Another Mexico by Graham Greene. Copyright 1939, © 1967 by Graham Greene. The excerpt appearing on pages 158–59 is reproduced by permission of The Viking Press, Inc.

"Atitlan," from *Beyond the Mexique Bay* by Aldous Huxley. Copyright © 1934, 1962 by Aldous Huxley. The excerpt on page 146 reproduced by permission of Harper & Row, Publishers, Inc.

Hernan Cortes. Letters from Mexico. Translated and edited by A. R. Pagden. Copyright © 1971 by Anthony Pagden. The excerpts appearing on pages 21 and 138–41 are reproduced by permission of Grossman Publishers.

Indian Art of Mexico and Central America by Miguel Covarrubias. Copyright © 1957 by Alfred A. Knopf, Inc. The excerpts appearing on pages 34 and 57 are reproduced by permission of Alfred A. Knopf, Inc.

Official Reports to His Majesty Philip II. Peabody Museum Papers, Volume 11, No. 2. The excerpt on pages 148–49 reproduced by permission of Peabody Museum Papers, Harvard University.

Selected Poems of Octavio Paz. Translated by Muriel Rukeyser. Copyright © 1963 by Muriel Rukeyser. The excerpt on page 159 reproduced by permission of Indiana University Press.

The Aztecs of Mexico by George D. Vaillant. Copyright © 1956 by George D. Vaillant. The excerpt appearing on page 51 is reproduced by permission of Doubleday & Co., Inc.

The Aztecs: The History of the Indians of New Spain by Fray Diego Duran. Edited and translated by Doris Heyden and Fernando Horcasitas. Copyright © 1964 by the Orion Press. The excerpt appearing on pages 142–43 is reproduced by permission of Grossman Publishers.

The Broken Spears: The Aztec Account of the Conquest of Mexico by Miguel Leon-Portilla. Copyright © 1962 by the Beacon Press; originally published in Spanish under the title of *Vision de los Vencidos;* copyright © 1959 by Universidad Nacional Autonoma de Mexico. The excerpt appearing on page 144 is reproduced by permission of Beacon Press.

The Discovery and Conquest of Mexico by Bernal Diaz del Castillo. Edited by Genaro Garcia. Translated by A. P. Maudslay. Copyright © 1956 by Farrar, Straus and Cudahy, Inc. The excerpt appearing on pages 141–42 is reproduced by permission of Farrar, Straus & Giroux, Inc.

The Plumed Serpent by D. H. Lawrence. Copyright © 1926 by Alfred A. Knopf, Inc. and renewed 1954 by Frieda Lawrence Ravagli. The excerpt appearing on pages 147–48 is reproduced by permission of Alfred A. Knopf, Inc.

The Prehistory of the Tehuacan Valley, Vol. I by Richard S. MacNeish. Copyright © 1967 by Richard S. MacNeish. The excerpt appearing on page 29 is reproduced by permission of the University of Texas Press.

The Editors would like to express their particular appreciation to Ada C. de Contreras at the Museo Nacional de Antropología in Mexico City, to Dr. Gordon Ekholm at the American Museum of Natural History in New York, to David Starbuck of Yale University for compiling the chronology of Mesoamerican history, and to Irmgard Groth and Doris Heyden in Mexico City for their invaluable assistance. In addition, the Editors would like to thank the following organizations and individuals:

Arte Primitivo, New York
  Mr. and Mrs. Allen Kaplan
Russell Ash, London
Jane de Cabanyes, Madrid
Hunt Botanical Library, Pittsburgh
  Katherine Daniels
Museo Nacional de Antropología, Mexico City
  Margarita de Laris

Dr. Arthur G. Miller, New Haven
Barbara Nagelsmith, Paris
Dr. and Mrs. Josué Sáenz, Mexico City
Lynn Seiffer, New York
Thelma Sullivan, Mexico City
Philip Teuscher, Weston, Connecticut
Sylvia Winsor, Rome

The title or description of each picture appears after the page number (boldface), followed by its location. Photographic credits appear in parentheses. The following abbreviations are used:

AMNH — American Museum of Natural History, New York
(IG)   — (Irmgard Groth)
MNAM — Museo Nacional de Antropología, Mexico City

ENDPAPERS New fire ceremony, from the *Codex Nuttall*. British Museum HALF TITLE Symbol by Jay J. Smith Studio FRONTISPIECE Wall painting of the quetzal bird, Teotihuacán. Dr. and Mrs. Josué Sáenz, Mexico City 9 Mosaic and shell funerary mask, Teotihuacán, Guerrero, A.D. 200–700. MNAM (IG) 10–11 Temple of Quetzalcoatl, Teotihuacán. (Philip Teuscher) 12–13 The Aztec god of war, from *Codex Borbonicus*. Bibliothèque du Palais Bourbon, Paris (Giraudon)

CHAPTER I 14 Stone ball game marker, from La Ventilla, Teotihuacán, A.D. 375–450. MNAM 16 Model offertory in patio at Atetelco. 16–17 Chambers at Tetitla. 17 Chambers at Atetelco. All: 16–17 (Philip Teuscher) 18–19 The Pyramid of the Sun and the Avenue of the Dead, Teotihuacán. (Philip Teuscher) 21 Statue of Tlaloc being transported to Mexico City, 1964. (Jorge Cabrera) 23 Statue of Tlaloc at Museo Nacional de Antropología, Mexico City. (Irmgard Groth)

CHAPTER II 24 Pottery female figurine from Tlatilco, 1100–500 B.C. MNAM (IG) 26–27 Three plates from Leonhard Fuchs's *De Historia Stirpium*, Basel, 1542. Hunt Botanical Library, Pittsburgh 28 Pottery dog with corncob, Colima, 8–10th century. MNAM 29 left, Pottery figure of a woman using a metate, Colima, A.D. 100–500. MNAM; right, Stone figure of a man holding a squash, Veracruz, 14th century. Brooklyn Museum 31 Pottery vase in shape of an acrobat, Tlatilco, 1100–500 B.C. MNAM 32 Pottery bowl in shape of a fish, Tlatilco, 1100–500 B.C. MNAM (IG) 32–33 Pottery figurines of the Preclassic era. Heye Foundation, Museum of the American Indian 33 Top right, Pottery head of a female figurine, Tlatilco, 1100–500 B.C. MNAM (IG); bottom left and right, Two pottery figurines, Tlatilco, 1100–500 B.C. MNAM (IG) 34 Pottery mask, Tlatilco, 1100–600 B.C. MNAM 35 Pottery figurine of a woman with a dog, Tlatilco, 1100–600 B.C. MNAM (IG)

CHAPTER III 36 Jadeite ax, Olmec, 700–600 B.C. AMNH 38 Jadeite mask, Olmec, c. 1300 B.C. MNAM 39 Pottery figurine of a child-man, Olmec, 1300–800 B.C. Museum of Primitive Art (Lisa Little) 40 Stone sculpture, *The Wrestler*, Olmec, Santa María Uxpanapa, 1100–500 B.C. MNAM (IG) 41 Stela C, Olmec, Tres Zapotes, 31 B.C. MNAM 42 Tomb A from La Venta, Tabasco. Museo Parque La Venta, Villahermosa, Tabasco (Irmgard Groth) 43 top, Wooden mask, Olmec, Guerrero, 1150–950 B.C. AMNH; center, Stone head, Olmec, Veracruz, 1100–500 B.C. MNAM (IG); bottom, Jadeite jaguar-baby, Olmec, Puebla, 1150–500 B.C. AMNH 44 Pottery figure wearing jaguar skin, Olmec, Morelos, 1100–900 B.C. 45 Mosaic floor from La Venta, Tabasco. Museo Parque La Venta, Tabasco (Irmgard Groth) 46 Stone apelike sculpture, Olmec, 500 B.C.–A.D. 200. Museo Parque La Venta, Tabasco (Irmgard Groth) 47 Stone head, Olmec, San Lorenzo, MNAM 48–49 Jadeite ritual cache, Olmec, La Venta, Tabasco, 850–400 B.C. MNAM (IG)

CHAPTER IV 50 Pottery statue of Xipe Totec, Teotihuacán, A.D. 600–900. MNAM (IG) 52 Pottery seated man, Teotihuacán, c. A.D. 250–375. MNAM 53 left, Jadeite figurine from Offering 2, Temple of Quetzalcoatl, A.D. 250–650. MNAM (IG); right, Pottery figurine, Teotihuacán, A.D. 150–250. MNAM (IG) 55 Map of Teotihuacán, by René Millon, University of Rochester, all rights reserved 56 Onyx funerary mask, Teotihuacán, A.D. 400–600. MNAM (IG) 58–59 Two wall paintings from Zacuala and the Avenue of the Dead, Teotihuacán (Both: Dr. Arthur G. Miller) 60–61 Three reliefs from the Butterfly Palace, Teotihuacán, A.D. 250–650 (All: Philip Teuscher) 62 top, Thin Orange foot, Teotihuacán, A.D. 400–600. MNAM; center, Thin Orange bowl, Teotihuacán, A.D. 400–600. MNAM; bottom, Thin Orange tripod bowl with jaguar, Teotihuacán, A.D. 250–600. MNAM   **62–63** Thin Orange dog, Teotihuacán, A.D. 250–600. Dr. and Mrs. Josué Sáenz, Mexico City   **63** top, Thin Orange reclining man, Teotihuacán, A.D. 250–600. MNAM (IG); bottom, Fragment of a Thin Orange bowl, Teotihuacán, *c.* A.D. 450. MNAM   **64** Pottery figure, Zapotec, Monte Albán, *c.* 300–200 B.C. Museo Regional de Antropología, Oaxaca (Irmgard Groth)   **64–65** Monte Albán. (MNAM)   **65** upper right, Pottery funerary urn, of Xipe Totec, Zapotec, Monte Albán, A.D. 600–1000. MNAM; bottom, Relief, *Danzante,* Zapotec, Monte Albán, 500–200 B.C. (Irmgard Groth)   **66** Jade and shell mask of bat god, Zapotec, Monte Albán, 200 B.C.–A.D. 200. MNAM (IG)   **67** Pottery funerary urn of a jaguar, Zapotec, Monte Albán, 200 B.C.– A.D. 200. MNAM (IG, courtesy Thames & Hudson)   **68** Reconstructed tomb from the Temple of the Inscriptions, Maya, Palenque. MNAM (IG)   **68–69** Palenque. (Mexican Government Tourist Office)   **69** Lintel over Door 26, Maya, Yaxchilán, A.D. 726. (Irmgard Groth)   **70–71** Three reconstructions of the Bonampak murals, Maya. All: MNAM   **73** top, Pottery figurine of woman with codex, Maya, Jaina. A.D. 550–900. MNAM; bottom, Detail of *Codex Tro-Cortesianus,* Maya. Museo de America, Madrid (Oronoz)   **74** Pottery woman with headdress, Maya, Jaina, A.D. 550–900. MNAM (IG)   **75** top left, Pottery ballplayer, Maya, Jaina, A.D. 550–900. MNAM; top right, Pottery dignitary, Maya, Jaina, A.D. 550–900. MNAM; bottom left, Pottery man with hat, Maya, Jaina, A.D. 550–900. MNAM; bottom right, Pottery man, Maya, Jaina, A.D. 550–900. AMNH

CHAPTER V   **76** Two stone totems, Toltec, Tula, A.D. 968–1168. (Mexican Government Tourist Office)   **79** Stone warrior from Temple of Quetzalcoatl, Toltec, Tula, A.D. 856–1168. MNAM (IG)   **80** Mother-of-pearl coyote, Toltec, Tula, *c.* 11th century. MNAM   **81** top, Gold and turquoise pectoral, Mixtec, Yanhuitlán, A.D. 1300–1521. MNAM (IG); left, Gold earring, Mixtec, A.D. 1300–1521. Museum of Primitive Art (Lisa Little); bottom, Gold pectoral, Mixtec, Tapantla, A.D. 1300–1521. MNAM (IG)   **82** Stone statue of Xochipilli, Aztec, Tlalmanalco, A.D. 1440–1521. MNAM (IG)   **83** Stone calendar, Aztec, Mexico City, *c.* 1479. MNAM   **84–85** The Aztec journey, from *Histoire Mexicaine,* 59–64, fol. 5. Bibliothèque Nationale, Paris   **87** Wooden drum, Aztec, Malinalco, A.D. 1440–1521. MNAM   **88** Aztec calendar, from *Codex Borgia,* Messicano 1, fol 30, Biblioteca Vaticana   **90–91** Aztec sacrifice, from *Codex Magliabecchiano,* Biblioteca Nacional, Florence (Loubat copy, Library of Congress)   **91** Stone jaguar, Aztec, Tenochtitlán, A.D. 1440– 1521. MNAM   **92** Aztec ball game, from *Codex Magliabecchiano.* Biblioteca Nacional, Florence (Loubat copy, Library of Congress)   **93** Chichén Itzá. (Irmgard Groth)   **94** Mask of Tezcatlipoca, Aztec, A.D. 1440–1521. British Museum   **94–95** Mask of Tlaloc, Aztec, A.D. 1440–1521. National Museum, Copenhagen   **95** Mask of Quetzalcoatl, Aztec, A.D. 1440–1521. British Museum

CHAPTER VI   **96** Stone palma of bundled arrows, Veracruz. MNAM (IG)   **98** Hernán Cortés, from Christoph Weiditz's *Trachtenbuch . . . ,* Nuremberg, 1529. Germanisches Nationalmuseum, Nuremberg   **99** Map of Tenochtitlán, from Hernán Cortés's *Praeclara Ferdinadi. . . ,* Nuremberg, 1524. Rare Book Division, New York Public Library   **101–02** Six episodes from Bernardino de Sahagún's *Historia de las Cosas De Nueva Espana, Codex Fiorentino,* Ms. Pal. 220. Biblioteca Laurenziana, Florence   **102–03** Cortés and his legions, from *Histoire Mexicaine,* Ms. Mexicain 90, fol 44. Bibliothèque Nationale, Paris   **105** Cortés on horseback, from *Ms. Vaticanus A,* Latin 3738, fol 87r. Biblioteca Vaticana, Rome   **106** Map by Francis & Shaw, Inc.   **107** Aztec chieftain, from *Histoire Mexicaine,* Ms. Mexicain 59–64, fol 12v. Bibliothèque Nationale, Paris   **108** Sacrificial knife, Aztec, 1440–1521. British Museum   **109** Moctezuma, from Diego Durán's *Historia de las Indias . . . .* Biblioteca Nacional, Madrid (Oronoz)   **110–11** top, Cortés in Tlaxcala; bottom, Alvarado fighting Aztecs. Both: Durán's *Historia de las Indias . . . .* Biblioteca Nacional, Madrid (Oronoz)   **112** Two drawings of Moctezuma, from the *Codex Fiorentino,* Ms. Pal. 219–20. Biblioteca Nacional, Florence   **113** Moctezuma's death, from *Codex Fiorentino,* Ms. Pal. 220, 447v. Biblioteca Laurenziana, Florence.   **115** Spaniards approach village, from *Ceremonias y Ritos de los Indios de Mechuacan,* 1540–41. Biblioteca Escorial.   **116–17** Post-Columbian map of Teotihuacán. AMNH

CHAPTER VII   **181** Pottery funerary urn of maize god, Zapotec, Oaxaca. Musée de l'Homme, Paris   **120** Frescoed vase, Teotihuacán, A.D. 400–700. Gift Mrs. George H. Bunting, Jr., Nelson Gallery-Atkins Museum.   **123** Engraving of Uxmal, from Frederick Catherwood's *Views of Ancient Monuments . . . ,* London, 1844, Rare Book Division, New York Public Library   **124–25** Engraving of Palenque, from Frederick Catherwood's *Views of Ancient Monuments . . . ,* London, 1844. Rare Book Division, New York Public Library   **127** Stela D, Maya, A.D. 766, Quirigúa, Guatemala. (Maudslay Collection, British Museum)   **129** Pottery vase of a turkey. Teotihuacán, A.D. 250–375. MNAM   **130–31** Teotihuacán in 1895. (Heye Foundation, Museum of the American Indian)   **132** Pottery censer, Teotihuacán, A.D. 450–750. Gift of Joseph Antonow, Art Institute of Chicago   **135** Palace of Quetzalcoatl, Teotihuacán. (Philip Teuscher)

ANCIENT MEXICO IN LITERATURE   **136** The founding of Tenochtitlán, from the *Codex Mendoza,* 1541. Bodleian Library, Oxford   **138–60** Scenes of Aztec life, from Bernardino de Sahagún's *Historia de las Cosas de Nueva Espana, Codex Fiorentino,* Biblioteca Laurenziana, Florence

REFERENCE   **165** Map by Francis & Shaw, Inc.

Index